PRIVATE HELL

by Donna M. Carbone

We are all dead and just don't know it
Heaven and Hell are the same place
Bliss is impermanent
Punishment is eternal

Private Hell is a semi-autobiographical account of my life from birth to the present. I've known pain. I've known joy. Despite what you might think, I am grateful even to those people who caused me to suffer deeply. Without them I would not value joy with equally deep intensity. Without them, I would not be the person I am today. Pain made me strong. Joy softened the edges and allowed me to grow into someone proud and self-sufficient.

There are people in my life whom I remember fondly and with deep gratitude not because they are related by blood but because they risked their own lives to prevent my blood from being spilled. My husband of 41 years stands tall among them. He has not only my love but my undying gratitude. During the early days of our marriage when trust was in short supply, he allowed me to heal at my own pace. He never asked for more than I could give. He was supportive and kind and patient when most people would have run for the door. He was, is, and always will be the wind beneath my wings.

My sister, Joan, is one of my heroes. Nine years older than I, she often fulfilled the role of mother as we were growing up. Later, when my life was threatened by circumstances beyond my control, she put her own life and that of her family in jeopardy to keep me safe. There are no words which can express the depth of my love for her and the gratitude I feel in my heart.

There were other people along the way... an employer who was loving, patient and kind during the most trying period of my life... family members and friends who opened their arms and their doors when my world was crumbling around me... strangers who interceded without thought for their own safety. Some of them have moved on to that "better place." Some I have not heard from or seen in decades. They have not been forgotten. There is rarely a day that passes when I don't think of them and offer a silent "Thank you."

If you know someone who is being victimized by domestic violence, please, extend a hand. Let them know that you are there to help in whatever way possible. A smile... a kind word... a hug... any small sign that you understand and care can be a lifeline in the roiling sea that is abuse. Many times those who are most in need appear to be the least in need. Look below the surface. You will be rewarded for your efforts.

Donna M. Carbone

Also by Donna M. Carbone

Crime Novels:

The Cat Leigh and Marci Welles Crime Series –

Through Thick and Thin
Silk Suit/Stone Heart (Dec. 2016)

Mysteries:

Private Hell

True Stories:

Assault on an Angel – A Rape Survivor's Story

Stage plays:

Shell of a Man
Women, Wisdom and Wine
Pluck You!
Soul Searching
Fear Sells

Private Hell is a work of fiction. Names, characters, business-es, organizations, events and incidents either are the product of the author's imagination or are used fictitiously. Any references to historical events, real people, living or dead, or real locales are used fictitiously.

For information, contact:
Write For You, LLC
Palm Beach Gardens, Florida 33410
www.writeforyoullc.com

Acknowledgements

To my husband Mike, my son Michael and daughter-in-law Leah, my daughter Jessica and son-in-law Kevin, my grandson Blake and my new granddaughter, Everest. You are the fulfill-ment of my dreams – no wife/mother/grandmother could ask for a better family.

I love you all so very much!

I would also like to thank my good friend and favorite beta reader, Kathy Banfield, who has spent countless hours reading and re-reading every chapter of this book looking for typing and spelling errors, inconsistencies, and just plain dumb mistakes. She makes me look good!

Special thanks to my daughter, Jessica, whose amazing pho-tographs grace the covers of all my books and to Kevin Mayle, a design master extraordinaire, who created the covers for *Private Hell* and *Through Thick and Thin*.

View Kevin Mayle's work at:
http://kevinmayle.webs.com/apps/photos/

by Donna M. Carbone

Mirror Image

Reflections distorted by the dust of our lives
The minutes, the hours, the years
Images cleansed to be covered again
By deception, hopelessness and fear

Donna M. Carbone
2009

PROLOGUE

2015

"I don't worry about whether there's a God or a heaven or hell. I don't crave eternal reward or fear eternal punishment. I live a good life because I wouldn't be able to look at myself in the mirror if I didn't. If, when this suitcase we call a body, wears out, I find that there is a God, I'm sure he or she or it will know I was a decent human being. So... I'm not afraid to die. I just don't want to die now."

Victims' Rights attorney Claudia Allerd sat behind her desk making mental notes on the conversation she just had with a new client. Shocked by what she had learned, the telephone receiver was still in her hand. Former spouses wanting to kill their exes was nothing new. Allerd had heard hundreds of stories in her long career—many of them bizarre, sometimes perverse, almost all of them high profile and dealing with women's issues. Her passion for defending her gender was the direct result of being sexually assaulted while on vacation at a resort in Mexico. The rape, which like many women she never reported, led to a pregnancy and an abortion. Since abortions were illegal at the time, the procedure was done under less than optimal conditions. Hemorrhaging, infection and a brush with death followed. The experience left the then twenty-two year old profoundly aware of how unfairly women were treated, especially when it came to making decisions about their bodies and lives.

In her 30 year career, Allerd had represented clients from all walks of life. Her services were available to everyone regardless of race, gender, age, sexual orientation, social status or ability to pay. Many of her cases were civil suits running the gamut of sexual harassment, assault, wrongful termination, individual and family right, employment discrimination, and, of course, cases that promoted the legal and social equality of women and minorities. No one and nothing intimidated her. She was not above using theatrics to make her viewpoints known. When the State of California was considering outlawing abortions, she presented the senator who had authored the bill with a Renaissance period chastity belt in full view of the sitting legislature. The media ran with the story, and Allerd became a household name. From that moment on, her face was instantly recognizable to television news watchers. Her photograph often graced the front page of major newspapers. She used her celebrity to further her clients' chances of victory whenever possible. If Claudia Allerd called a press conference, the world stopped turning long enough to watch and listen.

Whenever trouble reared its ugly head, everyone - the famous, the infamous and the unpresuming – found their way to Allerd's door. Those seeking her services included people suspected of committing murder, those on the receiving end of death threats, and the actual dead. Rarely surprised by the who and what of a case, Allerd found Diana Ciccone's story intriguing. It involved a physically and emotionally dysfunctional childhood, domestic abuse which had begun when Ciccone was in her teens and which now, at the age of 66, had morphed into stalking and the strong potential for a headstone with her name on it.

Picking up a copy of Ciccone's novel, *Private Hell,* Allerd ran her finger down the cover. The photo depicted a rose laying atop a mirror; it's reflected image a perfect copy with one exception. The original rose was red. The reflected rose was blackened and dying. Imprinted below the photo were the words, "Sometimes heaven and hell are the same place." Allerd agreed but, based on her experiences, she was inclined to believe that hell held dominance over the phenomenon called life.

Ciccone's book had arrived by special delivery in the morning's mail. The note attached was enough to spur an internet search of the author; the results of which further piqued Allerd's interest. According to the bio on the book jacket, Ciccone had escaped an abusive mother and ineffectual father by marrying her high school sweetheart. The marriage resulted in a jumping from the frying pan into the fire type of existence. Her survival was a miracle made possible by the intervention of family members willing to jeopardize their own lives to hide and protect her.

Time passed and with it the threats to her life seemed to fade away. When in her mid-twenties, Ciccone remarried and her life became the stuff of fairy tales... a handsome husband, two wonderful children, a beautiful home... all her dreams had come true. She was happy, safe, recognized in her community for being charitably active and, like many mature women, was currently using her retirement years to pursue a new career.

Diana Ciccone had always wanted to be a writer. She decided to use a fictional account of her early years of abuse as the basis for a crime drama. The book was a huge, unexpected success. Although she had authored it using the pseudonym Marjorie Markel, her true identity became known far and wide. Her ex-husband, up to now a sleeping bear, had been poked. He was not happy. The past had found its way into the present. Ciccone's life was once again in danger. She needed help.

Claudia Allerd was a successful attorney because she was meticulous in her research and formulated a battle plan for every probable eventuality. Her attention to detail in preparing for courtroom skirmishes had paved the road to many ground breaking decisions which forever changed the way people lived their lives. When taking on a new case, she fully immersed herself in her client's life. With the intent of knowing Diana Ciccone better than Ciccone knew herself, Allerd buzzed her legal assistant and told her to hold all calls. Then, *Private Hell* in hand, she settled in for a day of reading.

CHAPTER ONE

1973

With the public address system announcing, "Ten minutes til closing," Palma hurriedly gathered up her pocketbook, notepad, cell phone and umbrella, performing a circus-perfect balancing act as she rushed to the checkout counter. In her arms, she cradled the week's selections—two books describing the beauty of the Tuscan countryside and another detailing the magnificent works of Michelangelo. The fourth book, a dog-eared and oft read copy of Taber's Cyclopedic Medical Dictionary, was buried beneath the stack and seemed oddly out of place with her other choices.

The illustrated medical text dealing with surgery, nursing, dietetics and drugs was copyrighted 1965. No doubt much of the information contained between its worn green and gold binding was outdated. Nonetheless, Palma seemed pleased with her findings. A yellow post-it note, marking the annotated section dealing with anatomical and physiological emergencies, stuck out from near the back of the book. On a separate pad, carefully copied notes had been written in Palma's precise hand. The use of a ruler kept her cursive absolutely straight and attested to the detail she focused on every project she undertook. Two underlined and emboldened words headed the columns at the top of the lined sheet of paper: Symptoms and Treatments.

Symptoms	Treatments
Apprehension	Quiet
Stiffness of muscles	Cool, dark room
Twitching of face/arms	Avoid drafts
Convulsions	Avoid choking on tongue
Difficulty breathing	tracheotomy
Death	None

Two additional columns—How and Where (to find)—were empty. Written almost as an afterthought were two words: castor beans.

**

2 tablespoons olive oil
2 cloves garlic – minced
1 sweet onion – minced
½ dry red wine
2 teaspoons dried oregano
1 teaspoon dried basil
2 bay leaves – whole
Pinch of sugar
Crushed red pepper to taste
Crushed tomatoes
Salt and Pepper to taste

Amber streaks of sunlight pierced the window as the slowly disappearing sun settled in for the night. Diffused by the rain streaked glass, the rays illuminated the kitchen with an iridescent glow. Palma watched transfixed as the somewhat eerie shimmer faded away, turning the room from other-worldly to ordinary. Slipping a chef's apron over head to protect her antique lace blouse and well-worn form fitting jeans, she slow danced around the kitchen, gathering up the ingredients for her grandmother's special sauce. Although she had prepared this recipe on many, many occasions, she was nervous. On this night, everything had to be perfect.

As Palma whirled gracefully about the room, moving from pantry to counter top to stove, the lacy texture of the blouse, soft with age, teasingly brushed her arms like a finger gently stroking her skin. The sheer fabric of the low cut shirt, ruffled just above her breasts, was demurely feminine while the well-worn and faded jeans encasing her long legs spoke of comfort and ease. Together, they created an impression of casual elegance. With carefully applied makeup enhancing her high cheekbones and full lips, Palma was every man's seduction fantasy.

Little about her birth would Palma consider a blessing, but the combination of her mother's delicate beauty and her father's height and lean physique was a gift; one she had not fully appreciated until she entered the business world. Combined with a natural intelligence and a large measure of common sense, she was a formidable package with which to reckon. Her current job provided not only financial security but also gave Palma the unwavering acceptance that she had been seeking for so long.

Curvy and statuesque at nearly six-feet-tall, Palma Domenica Rigo, so named because she had been born on Palm Sunday, towered over other women and some men. She carried her height proudly—spine straight, shoulders back, head held high. Her pale skin, vivid blue eyes and shoulder length natural blond hair had often been the cause of jealousy, making close female relationships a rarity. Only extremely confident women were not threatened by her presence... the kind of women she now called friends.

Those who made an effort to know Palma soon realized that under the movie star looks was an unaffected, sane, sensible woman who valued honesty, charity and loyalty above all other external marks of distinction. She believed in giving a full day's work for a full day's pay, and she spent her hard earned money wisely. Given the choice between an expensive gourmet dinner at the Waldorf Astoria and a Nathan's Hot Dog, she always chose the dog. Not one to primp, Palma was often startled by the beauty of the face staring back at her from the mirror. She thought of herself as just an average girl.

How Palma envisioned herself was very different from the assumptions people made when meeting her for the first time. More often than not, opinions were formed based solely on her appearance; the relationship doomed before a word was spoken. Her teen years were a lonely and isolating experience, made more so by her dysfunctional home life. Girls envied her; boys were intimidated by her; and her mother resented her.

Competition among her peers was understandable, but her mother's jealousy was unnatural. So rarely had Palma heard words of praise that she had never been able to accept a sincere compliment without insisting it was undeserved. For three and a half years she had been a loner by circumstance not by choice. Each day she had crossed the quad feeling angry eyes boring into her back. Nasty, unfounded remarks followed the hateful stares. Teenage girls with shaky self images treated her like a pariah, claiming she was just too "uppity" to be one of them. The boys, convinced she would never date them, needed to assuage their sensitive egos by demeaning her with foul comments and sexual suggestions. Safe within their insular world, they had not realized that Palma's only defense was to hold her head higher and pretend she did not care what they thought of her. She often wondered whether, had they known that she longed to join their happy clique and listen to their stories of parties and dates, they would have accepted her. Her conclusion was always that they would not. The knowledge that Palma needed them would have stoked their simmering resentments and heightened their intended cruelty. So, each day she sat with the other ostracized souls and ate her sandwich in quiet contemplation—until senior year.

Senior year of high school had been the beginning and the end of her education on so many levels. The journey from then to this evening had been long, arduous and life threatening.

CHAPTER TWO

The two bottles of merlot purchased for this night's meal were still wrapped in the brown paper bag from the store. The temptation to open one was strong, and Palma decided that a glass would help to settle her nerves. She removed both bottles from the sack and placed one on the beautifully set dinner table. With a practiced hand, she opened the other bottle, removed the skewered cork and gave it a quick glance before placing it on the counter. She was informed enough to know that a dry cork was indicative of a bottle that had been stored improperly.

Palma took a tumbler from the dish cabinet and poured herself a small sampling of the wine. She inhaled the bouquet. Although she found this practice to be a sign of haughtiness, she did enjoy the heady scent of a newly opened bottle of good red wine. She sipped from the glass, relishing the taste and weight of the liquefied grape as it enveloped her tongue and trickled down her throat. Immediately, she felt warm and relaxed.

Not one to ignore a lesson learned, Palma grudgingly put down the glass before it was empty. She was aware that too much wine made her sleepy, and the last thing she wanted to do was reenact one of the most embarrassing moments of her life. She cringed thinking about that night just two weeks earlier.

***

The custom at the accounting firm where Palma worked was to celebrate each birthday with cake and coffee during the mid-afternoon break. Everyone in the department was invited whether they knew the celebrant or not. The birthday boy on this occasion was T.J. Perhamus, a fun, convivial sort who gave new meaning to the term "partee." After the usual off key singing of *Happy*

Birthday, someone in the group of ten told a humorous anecdote about his recent birthday, which encouraged another colleague to tell his "I'll never live it down" tale. A marathon of "I can beat that" stories ensued, forcing the partiers to shush each other as their language and laughter filled the corridor outside the break room. The blue ribbon for most riveting moment went to Louisa May, the office file clerk, who held everyone jaw dropped with her birthday revenge story.

Louisa May and her boyfriend of two years, Josh, had planned a four-day cruise to celebrate her 30th birthday. The trip was a gift from him to her, but the relationship had ended one month before departure when Louisa May discovered Josh in bed with another woman. As the deposit was non-refundable, the now ex-love of her life decided to travel alone, hoping to engage in a few one night stands. Louisa May was devastated by the breakup, but she got even in the most unlikely of ways.

At dinner the first evening at sea, a birthday cake blazing with candles and inscribed *Happy Birthday Louisa May* was delivered to the table Josh shared with a married couple and their two young sons. Since there was no Louisa May, he was forced to explain why he was alone. Too stunned to lie, he told the truth, perhaps, for the first time in his life.

The story spread and Josh was branded a cad by his fellow travelers. No single woman would have anything to do with him and his original dinner companions asked to be reassigned to a different table. Josh's new table mates were a virtue preaching minister, his wife and mother-in-law. As icing on the cake, the minister's mother-in-law turned out to be best friends with Louisa May's mother. Retribution was a gift that never got old as evidenced by the smile that spread across Louisa May's face at the end of the story.

The 15-minute break became a half hour and still no one wanted to go back to work. Each person had a story to tell; each trying to one-up the previous story teller. When a manager stuck his head in the door and raised his eyebrows to question the long delay in returning to their desks, they all agreed to continue the impromptu party at The Cantina, a popular Mexican eatery in the building's lobby at the end of the business day.

Palma had her own embarrassing story to tell, but it could not compare to the one yet to unfold. At 5:15 pm, the group met at the elevator and descended together, prepared for a fun night. Gathered around a large table in the middle of the restaurant, they talked over and around each other trying to be heard and to hear all that was being said. Pitchers of sangria and bottles of wine were delivered before the dinner orders were placed. One glass… two glasses… Palma had rarely felt so uninhibited. Listening and laughing until tears ran down her cheeks, she hung on her companions' words while waiting for her turn to speak. She did not notice how much she drank until lethargy overtook her.

The first outward sign of trouble was her withdrawal from conversation. Her sudden quietness went unnoticed due to the raucous nature of the diners. Slowly, her eyes began to close. Palma fought to stay awake, shifting in her chair and massaging her temples, but the feeling that someone was forcing her lids closed was overwhelming.

Suddenly, she felt the pressure of hands on her back and heard her name being called over and over again. Dazed, Palma opened her eyes and instantly realized that half of her face was resting in Combination Plate No. 6. Sheepishly, she raised her head. Her colleagues stared at her with concern and barely veiled amusement. Quickly grabbing her napkin, she wiped the residue of rice and beans from her cheeks and hair, pushed back her chair and ran for the ladies room.

Mortified but once more looking professional, Palma stoically returned to the table. Her office friends, a good natured bunch who knew the value of not casting stones, welcomed her back like a returning war hero. With overly large gestures, they raised their glasses and saluted her. "To Palma, the best storyteller and she hasn't yet said a word."

***

The embarrassment of that evening still fresh in her mind, Palma put down her glass and opened the pantry. Tucking cans of fire roasted tomatoes and jars of dried herbs into the crook of her arm, she mentally checked off ingredients—olive oil, garlic, basil, oregano, crushed red pepper. She would still need a little of the wine for the sauce and, perhaps, just a little more for herself.

A sip... just a sip... Palma promised herself as she reached for the tumbler. Raising it to her lips, she paused to appreciate the intensity of the wine's rich color. Deep red and seen through the faceted design, the glass resembled a huge ruby. One more sip and Palma was fortified with liquid courage. As she turned away, she caught her reflection in the door of the microwave. Sexy! Her confidence returned.

Luciano Pavarotti's amazing voice soared from the stereo in the living room, serenading Palma with sensually evocative lyrics. The music from La Boeheme was more intoxicating than the wine. Palma considered Pavarotti to be one of the most talented opera singers. In a less than pitch perfect voice, she sang along as she placed her armload of ingredients on the counter.

A person would have to be tone deaf, Palma knew, to call the flat screeching sounds that pierced the air singing. She even hummed off key. When, as a teenager, she had sung along with the latest hits on the radio, her dad would cross his eyes and ask, "Palma, can you carry that tune out into the backyard and bury it, please. The shovel is in the cellar. Dig deep!"

At first Palma was deeply offended by her father's criticism of her vocal skills, but one look at his comical face and belly laughs erupted along with the admission that he was right. Still, when alone, she sang with abandon, pretending to be Barbra Streisand, Cher or Helen Reddy. On this night, grandiose hand gestures accompanied a smattering of Italian and some Italian sounding words as she delivered a divaesque standing room only performance for the sofa and loveseat in the living room. She bowed deeply in gratitude for the thunderous applause only she could hear. Then, she laughed like the child she had never been.

The first notes of the next song caught Palma's attention, abruptly ending her laughter and bringing a melancholy smile to her beautiful face. The duet between Mimi and Rodolfo was both beautiful and sad. It bespoke of impending death—a real fear for Palma.

With sagging shoulders she returned to the kitchen. Once again she picked up the wine glass and leaned her body against the counter as she sipped the woody blend and listened to the songs. She didn't understand all the words but the sentiment was unmistakable. As the last notes faded away, Palma turned back to the chore at hand.

CHAPTER THREE

Palma's devotion to all things Italian began only hours after her birth; the instant Nonna cradled Palma in her arms and cooed, "Bella. Bella." softly against her cheek. The smooth texture of her grandmother's lips and the sweet scent of her breath, conjuring up visions of plump, ripe apricots and peaches from the garden, always soothed Palma when she was distressed.

An avid reader and student of history, Palma immersed herself in tales of Italy's ancient past. Books on art, architecture, and literature stood like sentries on the end tables in the living room. Beautiful color photographs of St. Mark's Square in Venice, the Spanish Steps in Rome, the works of Leonardo di Vinci and the gardens at Villa Borghese adorned the covers.

Thanks to a group tour arranged by her employer, Palma had been able to realize her dream of visiting her ancestral home. For 12 days she had trekked through the streets of Rome, Bologna, Pisa, Florence, Venice and Milan. For 12 days she had been at peace.

While in Rome, Palma had visited the Coliseum. She had reverently touched the walls, remembering all who had died for their faith and the amusement of cruel and vicious emperors. Overcome by the presence of so much history, she had repeated over and over again, "The Coliseum! The Coliseum! I'm in the Coliseum!" She was oblivious to the tourists around her, but those standing near enough to hear her words nodded in understanding. In the catacombs, Palma had stood before the empty graves and spoken respectfully to the spirits of the deceased. "Perhaps, this is silly," she confided, "but I want to wish you peace and happiness. I hope there is a heaven and you are there."

Awestruck in the Sistine Chapel, she had walked with head upturned trying not to bump into the throngs of people devouring Michelangelo's masterpiece with their eyes. The magnificent treasures of the Vatican made her wonder why there was still hunger in the world when selling just one chalice, one painting, one sculpture would end all suffering. Inside St. Peter's Basilica, she had moved quickly toward The Pieta. A small replica of this beautiful statue depicting a mother's love and sorrow had once held a place of honor on Nonna's dresser. As a child, Palma had loved holding it while Nonna told the story of Mary, her son Jesus, and the gift of life he had given to save all mankind. Palma wished her mother had loved her as unselfishly as Mary loved Jesus and Jesus loved all people.

While most of her traveling companions ate their meals in famous restaurants, Palma enjoyed frequenting neighborhood bistros and dining with the locals. One meal, in particular, had been memorable. Along with three of her favorite colleagues, she had opted out of visiting the Roman Forum in favor of acquainting herself with the citizens of Roma. For many hours Palma, Paul and Patti walked the back streets and alleys, stopping to admire the items in store windows along the way. They bought a few bottles of wine to enjoy when back at the hotel. A shawl hanging in one shop's window caught Palma's eye. Richly embroidered in earth tones of rust, green and brown, the soft fabric reminded Palma of Nonna's descriptions of the autumn orchards in her hometown. She could not resist buying it and stated her plan to wear it to church the next day. When growling stomachs had finally forced the three friends to acknowledge their hunger, they stopped to examine the delicious assortment of food on display in the nearest tratorria window.

The refrigerated case at the front of the combination market and restaurant was filled with prepared entrees. Dried sausages hung like exclamation marks overhead. The spicy aroma of salami, cappacola and prosciutto filled the air. There were a variety of pasta dishes, including lasagna and ravioli — not the frozen kind found in supermarkets in the states but handmade — large and plump with fresh ricotta and seasonings. Thinly sliced eggplant rolatini and thick breasts of chicken, lightly coated in tomato sauce and topped with fresh mozzarella slices, looked mouth wateringly delicious. A few whole fish—the fresh catches of the day—had stared back at Palma with black, unseeing eyes.

Seen from the open doorway, barrels and mesh bags of almonds, hazelnuts and walnuts made an artful display in one corner of the room. Palma had squealed like a child when she saw the bin of dried chickpeas called ceci nuts. These had been her favorite treat growing up. Loaves of fresh bread—long and thin, round and fat, crispy and golden brown—lined the top of the counter which divided the market area from the casual dining room. The longer Palma and her companions stared into the case and inhaled the delicious aromas, the hungrier they had become.

From the restaurant's threshold the handsome face of a young, dark haired cameriere beckoned Palma, Paul and Patti to enter. The waiter was about 16 but trying hard to appear older. Dressed in black slacks and shirt with a stiffly starched bright white apron tied about his waist, he almost succeeded. Only the humor in his smile and his fidgety shuffling of his feet betrayed his youthful nervousness. "New job... first day... first customers. Americans!" His misgivings telegraphed from his eyes like tickertape at the bottom of a newscast. Since the customers were battling their own nerves, his fears were quickly put to rest.

Cameriere meant waiter and was one of the words Palma had practiced on the plane. While most everyone else slept, she spent a restless night memorizing common words and phrases that might be helpful during her vacation. After clipping a small battery powered light to the top of an Italian vocabulary book, she determinedly worked her way through 15 pages of conversation.

> *Dove l'albergo?* – Where is the hotel?
> *Parla inglese?* – Do you speak English?
> *Mi dispiace, ma non parlo bene l'Italiano.* – I'm sorry. I
> don't speak Italian very well.
> *Cameriere* – waiter

was located.

Attending Sunday mass was a priority for Palma and the Church of Mary Immaculata was within walking distance. The church bells rang at 6:00 a.m. and, wearing her beautiful new shawl, an exhausted Palma struggled to stay awake.

The ancient church, unadorned of gilt and gold, and the straightforward manner of the parishioners left no doubt that here lived hard working people. The mass was said in Latin, something Palma rarely heard any more. The altar was covered in a simple hand-embroidered white cloth and decorated with vases of flowers brought by the school children. The lingering scent of burnt offerings from hundreds of other masses and benedictions caressed Palma's nose. She had always loved the woody, somewhat smoky and peppery, fragrance of incense. As a child her favorite service had been the walking of the Stations of the Cross. Whenever the priest raised the thurible during the ceremony, she would bow her head in reverence and inhale deeply. The jangle of the chain holding the burner and incense boat added to the dignity and solemnity of the service, reminiscent of the cock crowing thrice at Christ's betrayal.

On that morning in Ponte Cieve, she offered a prayer of gratitude that her dream to visit Italy had been realized. Her heart sang, "I am here. In Italy, where my great grandparents, my grandparents and my mother were born." Italy! The country had influenced her every thought and action from infancy. What she ate. What she read. What she wore. The way she decorated her home. Art. Music. History. Always, Italy had been at the heart of her choices, placed there by Nonna, whose love continued to protect Palma years after her death.

As Palma bowed her head, she felt a tingle on the back of her neck, as though someone was whispering in her ear. She was not afraid. Nonna was always with her. "Venire, Palma. We pray now."

When Palma exited the church, Father Ori Valari was waiting to greet her. He spoke English haltingly but with exuberance; a stranger in his church being a rare occurrence. Father Ori had been inquisitive, asking Palma questions about herself and her travels. When he learned she was Italian and realized her sincere love for the country, he invited her and her traveling companions to attend a concert in the church hall that evening. Palma accepted. "This is the real Italy." Her whispered words were directed to the heavens. "Nonna, I am finally home."

Surprisingly, the concert was not presented in Italian nor was it presented by Italians. A performing arts groups from a high school in Florida had been invited by the cultural ministry to tour a number of cities and Ponte Cieve was among them. Palma was certain that most of the audience failed to understand the Broadway show tunes that were sung, but they enjoyed the music and laughed heartily at a silly number called the Chicken Dance.

To the tune of Swiss accordion player and songwriter Werner Thomas' *Der Ententanz*, the young ladies and men, all under 18 years of age and dressed in cream colored cocktail dresses and black tuxedos, clucked and flapped their arms like barnyard fowl while strutting their fine feathers. They jumped from the stage and danced among the audience until the loud clapping drowned out the music. Smiles as big as that of the Cheshire Cat beamed from every face.

After the concert, a spaghetti dinner was served by the women of the parish. A simple salad, bread and wine completed the meal. The parishioners were sensible people who did not spend wealth they did not have, but riches of the heart were plentiful and given freely. The laughter of the children was pure; the men were gregarious; their wives were warm and welcoming. Palma envied the contentment she saw on their faces. When the bus pulled out the following morning, Palma left a part of herself in Ponte Cieve.

Venice brought Palma closer to her family's roots in Trento. The snow frosting the peaks of the Apennines made her wistful for a real connection to the people and the land. Here, the food was truly reminiscent of Nonna's cooking—the nutty flavor of olive oil, fresh fruits and vegetables and, of course, fresh sea food. Her first taste of pasta al nivuro di siccia would never be forgotten because it was both delicious and unusual—pasta in black squid ink sauce. Polenta, a simple cornmeal dish which Nonna had prepared regularly, was served sautéed to a golden brown alongside the cured ham of the region. Palma was always amused by polenta's sudden elevation to gourmet status in stateside restaurants. Nonna had called it "Depression food" because it kept many people from starving during those bleak days of no jobs and little money.

Due to Trento's proximity to Austria, Nonna's recipe for polenta had a decidedly Tyrolean flair. She served the warm, soft cornmeal with salamini—a fat, moist, spicy sausage—and with sauerkraut. Leftover polenta was sliced and browned in butter, just as the restaurant had done, and served with thinly sliced Genoa salami. In the southern regions of Italy, it was customary to bake the polenta with a covering of tomato sauce. Although delicious, Palma preferred the natural undisguised flavor of the coarsely ground dried corn.

Italy's grip on Palma, strong before her trip, tightened after her return to the States. She read even more avidly and listened to language tapes instead of the radio hoping to move beyond the simple conversational phrases she had learned on the plane. She began frequenting authentic Italian restaurants so that she could relive the rustic and robust flavors she had savored while in country. Instinctively, she gravitated to the open and sincere nature of the Italian people who exemplified her grandmother's nurturing ways.

Each evening before she closed her eyes to sleep, Palma thanked Nonna for giving her roots. Her adoration of her grandmother was godlike. Nonna's death 20 years before had left a seven-year-old Palma feeling abandoned and fearful. She still grieved; the sharp pang of loss that had squeezed her young heart had never subsided.

CHAPTER FOUR

The snap and sizzle of onions and the aroma of garlic sautéing in imported olive oil permeated the small kitchen, stoking sad, yet comforting, memories. This kitchen -- Nonna's kitchen -- had been a veritable garden of herbal scents when Palma was a child. Oregano, basil, and garlic... the Holy Trinity of Italian cooking. When Nonna was alive, the kitchen had been a cozy and inviting place, warm with the heavy aroma of yeast three mornings a week. Mondays, Wednesdays and Fridays were baking days and the smell of fresh bread browning in the oven was an invitation for family and friends to visit.

Palma loved those mornings. In an old ceramic bowl, Nonna would mix together the flour, salt, water and yeast. She then set the bowl covered with an old dishtowel near the stove, where the heat from the gas burners helped it to rise. After a few hours, she would turn the soft dough out onto a floured board and knead it with her strong hands. Kneeling on the chair next to Nonna, Palma had her own board and piece of dough to knead. Together, they formed their loaves into smooth, round shapes and cut a deep X into the center of each before placing them side by side on corn meal covered baking trays and sliding them into the oven.

Winter had been Palma's favorite season of the year. It was comforting to know that, although snow was falling outside, inside she was warm and safe with Nonna. Her grandmother's kitchen was gone now and in its place was an unrecognizable space filled with fashionable cabinets and updated appliances -- one of her mother's many renovation projects. The room felt cold to Palma. Only Nonna's memory made her feel like she belonged. She would often envision Nonna standing at the old stove, now part of a landfill somewhere in New Jersey, leaning heavily on her cane with one hand, a wooden spoon in the other. The memory made her mouth and her eyes water both for her grandmother's special sauce and her lost childhood.

"Palma. *Veni. Mange.*" Zoom! Like a rocket, Nonna's voice would bring Palma running. "Nella. Nella." Nonna would laugh. "Don't I feed you enough?"

With a chuckle, Nonna plunged the wooden spoon into the big pot and scooped up a mouthful of sauce as Palma waited impatiently near the stove. Palma's job, which she had taken very seriously, was to taste the sauce and pronounce it, "Done." Holding her tiny hands under her chin to catch any drips, Palma would stick out her tongue to gobble up the warm, spicy gravy. "It's so yummy, Nonna," she would say, rubbing her lips tightly together and pursing her mouth for emphasis.

Nonna's ample physique puffed up at the compliment. Giving Palma a loving pat on the backside, she would steer her toward the table. "Sit, Nella. We eat."

Side by side they sat, shoulders brushing, enjoying their time together even more than the food. The young one and the old one -- a life beginning and a life ending -- united by blood, cemented with love. Meal time was story time.

"Nonna, tell," was all the encouragement needed for Palma's grandmother to regale her little granddaughter with picturesque tales of her youthful days in northern Italy. The colorful images of Nonna's childhood village and the charming and not so charming descriptions of her grandparents, parents and siblings were more vivid than any issue of National Geographic found on the bookrack at a doctor's or dentist's office. Nonna had spoken emotionally of the countryside—the mountains and valleys surrounding her home, the apple orchards, the lemon, olive, walnut and chestnut trees and the vineyards. She spoke of her mother, a kind, devoted woman for whom family was a priority, and her father, a volatile man who rarely showed affection and whose authority was never questioned. Nonna's brother, older by three years, had adored his little sister, whom he teased mercilessly but not unkindly.

Palma's favorite story was about Nonna's father, Palma's great grandfather who was called *Rossa Barba* (Red Beard) by all who knew him. Short of stature but big on temper, Red Beard proudly grew his carrot-colored facial hair long and bushy on his round weathered jowls. He was the town bully and could most often be found in the local tavern, drunk from imbibing too many glasses of grappa. Each evening near dinnertime, a teenaged Nonna was sent by her mother to bring her father home. As women were not welcomed in the tavern, Nonna would stand outside the door and call her father's name until she was hoarse.

"Papa, il pranzo e pronto. Per favore, a casa ora venire. Mama sta attendendo." (Dinner is ready. Please come home now. Mama is waiting.)

"Papa, per favore! Il pranzo e sulla tabella. Non possiamo mangiare senza voi." (Papa! Please! Dinner is on the table. We cannot eat without you.)

Eventually, fists raised and bellowing curses, Red Beard would stumble out the door. Nonna would follow close behind as he staggered home, ready to pick him up should he trip and fall on the cobblestones, which he did often. Unlike her 5'3" father, Nonna was tall, towering over her father by seven inches. She was strong, too, resembling her uncles on her mother's side of the family. As she grew older, Nonna grew weary of the nightly ritual. She knew it was only a matter of time before the balance of power would shift and she dreaded that day. One evening, after calling her father's name for almost an hour, Nonna entered the tavern. Ignoring the angry stares of the village men, she stood beside her father, who was playing pinochle, and respectfully delivered her mother's message.

When Red Beard refused to acknowledge her presence, Nonna pulled his chair away from the table. Reaching under his arms, she lifted him up out of the chair and tucked him against her rib cage like a package of freshly laundered blankets and sheets. She carried him home, kicking and cursing. Entering the house, Nonna put her father down and awaited her punishment. Whatever Red Beard had been thinking of doing, one look at his daughter's face stopped any inclination toward violence. Embarrassment guaranteed his silence. From that day forward, he was home early and sober.

Nonna enjoyed talking about her late husband, Palma's grandfather, best of all. Berardo, had been the love of her life. She often spoke of their courtship, the long walks they had taken in the hills above their town, his kindness toward her mother and tolerance of her father. Their wedding, though simple, had been the highlight of Nonna's young life.

"*Dio mio* smiled on Nonno and me," Nonna told Palma. "The sun was bright and warm but the mountain breeze blew cool and refreshing. Mama cooked all morning, making beef braciole and ravioli for the guests. The tables under the grape arbor were covered with white sheets and strewn with flowers from the garden and nearby fields. There were pitchers of wine homemade by Zio Dominic on the tables. He grew the grapes behind his house and, after they were harvested, he pressed them in a big, old wooden barrel fitted with a hand crank. When I was a little girl, the heavy scent of the fermenting grapes would make me feel light headed and giddy."

Nonna would always rise at this part of the story to show Palma how she had walked down the aisle, putting one foot in front of the other to keep from tripping on her dress. "I guess I looked a little bit like my papa after a night in the tavern," Nonna laughed and Palma laughed with her, imagining her no nonsense grandmother behaving in such a manner.

"I wore a simple white dress that Mama and Zia Dona sewed for me." Nonna continued with her story. "It was very long and brushed the ground when I walked. Mama teased me by saying that because I was so tall, they had had to buy extra material and sew for three days to finish in time for the ceremony. On our wedding day, Nonno looked so handsome. Molto bello! He wore a dark grey suit and a white shirt that had been stiffly starched and ironed. My papa gave him the black tie he had worn when he married mama."

Nonna's eyes would grow watery and her voice would turn to a whisper as she thought back to her wedding day. "Nonno was a cobbler. Usually, his old pants and shirt were covered with a leather apron. To see him dressed so fine was a great surprise. He even made himself a new pair of shoes, a luxury for someone who could repair his old shoes. The black leather shone in the sunlight. Nonno said he needed special shoes because walking beside me was the proudest moment of his life. He wanted all our guests to know that I was worth the price of good leather.

Five years later, after your mama and Zia Idalia were born, we came to America. I was *cuore spezzato*—heartbroken. Leaving my mama, papa, and brother was hard, but a better life was promised here. *La famiglia* in New York sent for us to come and work in their factory. America—she was a good place to live. We learned the language and we took the oath. *Siamo stati molti orgogliosi*. We were very proud."

Although Nonna had been in the United States for many years, she still pronounced America with a lingering Italian accent and no less pride than the day she became a citizen.

As tall and lean as Nonna had been as a young woman, roly poly best described her bent and aged torso. Her thinning skin, which was always cold, was covered in one of her hand crocheted cardigans; the sleeves pushed up to the elbows in summer and held tightly against her wrists with rubber bands in winter. The multi-colored intertwining threads of the sweater made an interesting pattern, like strands of spaghetti twirled on a fork. While the infant Palma napped in Nonna's arms, the sweater would be wrapped around her bare arms and legs, encasing her little body in a wooly cocoon so that she slept soundly, feeling safe and protected. When she got older, Palma liked to run her little fingers over the threads as though she was following a roadmap. She would ask Nonna, "Where does the road begin? Where will it end?"

Through her toddler years, Palma played quietly on the floor at Nonna's feet while she crocheted for hours. Tilting her head upward, Palma would watch Nonna's silver crowned profile bent in concentration over the skeins of yarn. The bobby pins that held her hair in a bun on top of her head would catch the sunlight and twinkle like stars. Hour after hour, the sound of the crochet needles clicking set the tempo for the day. The clicking ceased only long enough for Nonna to prevent her wire-rimmed glasses from sliding off her nose. With three fingers curled into the palm of her hand and her thumb placed against her chin, she would quickly push the glasses back into place, a stiffly pointed index finger making sure they fit just right. Then, smiling down at Palma, she would blow a kiss and say, "*Bambina. Bambina mia. Ti amo molto.*"

So strong were the memories of those moments that Palma closed her eyes in the hope of recapturing the love she felt. She mimicked her grandmother, pushing imaginary glasses onto the bridge of her nose. Then, she placed her index finger to her lips and threw a kiss heavenward.

Although Nonna's hands remained strong, as the years passed, crippling arthritis made it difficult for her to walk and bend. Regardless, each evening she and Palma would kneel to pray. "*Veni*, Palma. We pray now." Palma would drag the extra dining room chair from its place by the bedroom window to the side of Nonna's double bed. Then she held the rosary beads while Nonna grasped the back of the chair to lower herself into a kneeling position. The pain, permanently stamped into the deep creases around her mouth, was obvious, but Nonna never complained.

Taking the rosary from Palma, Nonna held the crucifix in her gnarled fingers and made the sign of the cross. Palma would do the same; her little hands copying the exact motions Nonna made. When Nonna's lips began silently reciting the first Hail Mary, Palma raised her eyes toward the ceiling and prayed, too. "Please, God, make Nonna well. Don't take her away to heaven. I need her here with me."

Despite Palma's prayers, Nonna grew weaker. She cooked

less often as standing became more difficult. The crochet needles lay quiet, stuck into the sleeve of an unfinished sweater. Too weak to get out of bed most days, Nonna's greatest pleasure was to have Palma curl up beside her, their hands clasped in mutual affection. Late one evening, paramedics came to the house and carried Nonna out on a stretcher. Palma heard her cry out in pain as the men struggled to maneuver the stretcher down two flights of steep stairs.

Palma knew the end had come. Nonna never cried and she never came home again. There had been no good-byes, no chance to say "I love you" one last time. Palma stopped praying.

Nonna's death propelled Palma into a realm far different from what most children experienced. Although only seven, she had been forced to grow up very quickly. Remembering how her life had changed, Palma signed deeply. She searched for and found Nonna's strength deep within herself. She heard her grandmother say, "*Veni*, Palma. We pray now," and she knew with certainty that she had the courage to face the evening ahead.

CHAPTER FIVE

To further protect her clothes from being splattered with to-mato juice, Palma covered each can with a kitchen towel before attaching the hand-held opener to the rim. Holding the cans at arm's length, she emptied them one by one into the pot. Careful not to cut her fingers, she folded the sharp edged lids into the cans before throwing them into the garbage just as Nonna had taught her to do. Then, she crushed the dried herbs between her fingers, releasing their pungent aromas, and added them to the sauce.

Mimicking her grandmother yet again, Palma waved her fin-gers under her nose enjoying the delectable scent of oregano. While she stirred the pot, the aromatics stirred old memories. So many lessons had been learned at the stove and not just about cooking. Palma often found herself repeating Nonna's words of wisdom as she grated, chopped and sautéed food for her meals. Nonna's favorite—the parable of the Good Samaritan—was also Palma's favorite.

"Always do good deeds, Palma. People don't always show that they need help. Watch and listen. A smile… a word… you could change a person's life."

On bread baking days, Nonna would remind Palma about the Miracle of the Loaves and Fishes. "Food is a gift from God, Palma. It nourishes the body and the soul. Remember always to share your blessings with others less fortunate." Faith, love and kindness—Nonna had lived her life on those principles.

Nonna's stories were not only from the bible. Palma had gig-gled until her stomach hurt the first time she heard the charlotte russe story. Not until she was older did she realize that the tale was her grandmother's attempt to explain why her daughter, Palma's mother, had not been the least bit motherly.

***

Adrianna was born in the Aldo Adige region of the South Tyrol, an autonomous Italian province which then belonged to Austria. Once almost entirely German speaking, the area was given to Italy by the Allies during World War I in exchange for their support in the war. To prove their dominance, the Italian army marched into the country and took control. The residents, including a pregnant Nonna and her three children, were forced to walk long days and nights across the Alps into German controlled territory. Adrianna spent some of her formative years in an internment camp—hungry, cold and longing for her home. The lessons she learned about survival, including the birth and burial of twin sibling sisters, left an indelible impression on her young mind.

Although a beautiful child, Adrianna's beginnings were less than auspicious. She had been born prematurely, her tiny body easily fitting into a shoe box. Her diminutive size had made her the center of attention. Before the war she had been spoiled and, despite Nonna's best efforts to keep her daughter humble, she had quickly become a narcissist. During the war... while she and her family were incarcerated... her beauty had been used to coax an extra piece of bread and a little more milk from the soldiers for herself and her siblings. It was impossible to refuse the little blonde, blue eyed angel with big dimples in her cheeks. All Adrianna had to do was shed a tear or bat her eyelashes and extra rations would appear.

As she grew, she began to act more and more like a prima donna. She took delight in reminding her mother, older sister and brother that if not for her, they would have starved. Whenever she strutted her haughty ways, Nonna would say, "*Que brutta*! How ugly you are! Pride is a sin, *mia figlia*. When you were born, your face was not so pretty. It was wizened, like a prune. We kept you hidden in a drawer when company came to visit. God can do that to you again. Be humble."

Adrianna would just laugh. She knew her mama had made up the story. She was pretty... very pretty. Everyone said so.

Adrianna was seven when the family emigrated from Europe. Settling into a new life in a new country in a strange city was difficult for a child who spoke no English. Adrianna's parents were busy adjusting as well. They had little time to pamper a spoiled child. There was a new language to learn and new labor skills to master. To provide food, clothing and housing for the family, they worked long hours in factories and in the streets, paving roads and doing construction.

The moment the family stepped on American soil, they became painfully aware that the streets were not paved with gold as they had been told. Adrianna's papa left the house they shared with distant relatives before the sun came up every morning so as not to be late for his job. Her mama sat for long, tedious hours at the sewing machine set up in the living room, stitching new clothes for people with money to spare, letting out seams, raising and lowering hem lines and making repairs. Since Idalia and Louis, Adrianna's older sister and brother, were in school all day, Adrianna was often left to her own amusements.

As the years passed, Adrianna grew more independent and feisty. She had an impulsive nature and a thirst for learning that seemed unquenchable. Every morning she walked alone to the park near her home. While other children played tag and rode up and down on the seesaw, Adrianna sat on the swings, watching and listening. She did not join in, preferring to remain on the sidelines while she studied all that she saw and heard.

Over and over she repeated words and phrases used by the children. She began to know each of them by name, to recognize the expressions they used and the games they played. She knew the bullies and their prey; the ones who shared their toys and the ones who broke toys. When she was ready to enter the playground hierarchy, she knew who to befriend and who to avoid.

Adrianna waited for just the right moment. She had long since decided which child was to be her first friend. When the dark haired girl with the big brown eyes was alone in the sand box, Adrianna sat down beside her. Hesitantly, she smile a hello. The chosen one, named Jeannie, smiled back and offered a shovel. The venture was a success!

The children unhesitatingly accepted Adrianna; she entranced the bullies and the bashful. An astute child, she had learned to use her looks to her advantage. Within a few months, Adrianna sounded and acted like her playground companions. Despite her small size, she became their quasi leader, standing up for the timid ones when the need arose. At home, she rarely spoke Italian and insisted that her parents and siblings speak to her only in English.

The more conversant Adrianna became, the more daring she became. She roamed farther and farther away from home but always stayed within the confines of her ethnically selective neighborhood. These were the days when parents had less need to be concerned about the safety of their children. The streets were safe and people looked out for one another.

Confident beyond her years, Adrianna spent hours visiting the local shopkeepers; the husbands and wives who sold meat, fish and produce. With her cherubic face and open smile, she was always welcomed. The butcher gave her a hot dog or a chunk of bologna and from the vegetable cart, an apple was proffered. Occasionally, the grocer would dig deep into the big wooden barrel of cured cucumbers and present her with a crispy sour pickle. Adrianna loved the smell of garlic and dill that clung to the barrel's wooden slats. She posed with the air of an ambassador as walked and waved to passersby while munching on the wax paper wrapped delicacy.

So well-informed was she that when shopping needed to be done, Adrianna's parents would ask for her opinion of which store to patronize. Adrianna had learned to barter for better prices by watching the women who shopped in the local markets and she used those skills expertly. She knew when fresh vegetables and meats had been delivered and when the milk and cream had gone sour. From lessons learned in the internment camp, she always put her own needs first, a motivation that defined her character her entire life.

It was customary for Nonna to send her youngest daughter to the bakery after mass on the first Sunday of every month to buy a dozen sweet rolls. The buns, as they were called, were a special treat for the family of five; one that Nonna carefully saved for by putting aside a little of the grocery money every week. The thirteen buns—there was always an extra when buying a dozen—were divided equally among parents and children... one each at breakfast, lunch and dinner. Since 13 could not be divided evenly by five, Nonna would claim to be too full after lunch and dinner so that there would be enough for the others to share. The buns were best eaten on the day they were bought. Left until morning, they would be hard and dry.

The bakery order had been recited so often, Adrianna knew it by heart—a dozen mixed buns, no lemon or prune, extra cheese. The assortment always included three cherry, three blueberry, three pineapple and four cheese. On one particular Sunday, the bakery case had held a new pastry, which caught Adrianna's eye and made her mouth water. Wrapped inside a cardboard tube was a round slice of sponge cake covered in whipped cream and topped with a strawberry. Adrianna had not known there was cake inside the tube. All she saw were the clouds of heavy cream and the bright red fruits sliced into fans and spread open on top.

So irresistible did the dessert look that Adrianna forgot what she had come to the bakery to buy. When the salesgirl asked for her order, she had simply pointed to the delectable mounds arranged in rows behind the glass.

"You want a charlotte russe?"

Adrianna nodded her head, not taking her eyes off the tray of heavenly treats. As the salesgirl slid the refrigerator case door closed, Adrianna opened her tightly clenched fist and let the money spill onto the counter. A few coins spun in circles before falling atop the dollar bill and quarters in the pile but Adrianna was unaware of their movement. She reached for the charlotte russe that the salesgirl was putting into a box and buried her nose and mouth in its sweet goodness. Whipped cream left a billowy mustache on her upper lip and white puffs on her nose. She was struggling to dig her fingers into the tube when another customer spoke to her.

"This must be your first charlotte russe. Let me show you how to eat it. Look under the tube. See the cake. Just push it up with your fingers."

When Adrianna saw the cake in the bottom of the tube and realized there was to be another treat, she decided that a charlotte russe had to be the best dessert ever created. Not until the salesgirl asked if she wanted anything else did she realize what she had done. The buns! Adrianna's face telegraphed embarrassment and shame.

"How am I going to buy the buns for my family?" She reached for the coins and bill she had dropped and began to count.

Quickly Adrianna's smiles turned to tears which flowed down her cheeks, washing away the cream that her tongue had not been able to reach. Thinking Adrianna was ill, the salesgirl rushed from behind the counter. Other patrons gathered about, each voicing their concern. Hiccupping and sobbing, Adrianna explained that she was supposed to buy a dozen buns—no prune or lemon, extra cheese—for her parents and siblings. They were going to be so disappointed and mama would surely be angry. "I don't know what to do."

Although sympathetic, the salesgirl could not give away the sweet rolls for free. The money on the counter would buy six buns—enough for her mother, father, sister and brother to enjoy. The look on Adrianna's face spoke volumes. "I will never eat a sweet roll or charlotte russe again without feeling sick." Hanging her head until her chin touched her chest, she asked the lady who had shown her the cake in the bottom on the tube, "How can something go from wonderful to terrible so quickly?"

Adrianna could not stop sniffling as she waited for her order. She thought about all the other times she had been naughty and realized that this was worse by far. She feared her mother would never forgive her. Engrossed in her own troubles, she did not hear the kindly customer whisper to the salesgirl, "Make it a baker's dozen. I'll pay for them."

Adrianna never noticed that the lady have moved to stand beside her until she felt a hand on her chin. The lady gently raised Adrianna's face and wiped her tears and the remaining whipped cream away with a handkerchief from her purse. "Go home, little one. Everything will be all right."

The lady lifted the wrapped package of buns from the counter and handed it to Adrianna with a smile. So heavy was Adrianna's grief, that she did not notice the weight of the package she now carried. Momentarily, she thought the package felt heavier than one containing only six buns should feel. The only explanation that made sense was that the guilt she was feeling must be weighing it down. She left the bakery and walked slowly home wishing for a miracle. While still a block from her house, she saw her mother standing at the front door, an anxious expression on her face.

"Adrianna, why did you take so long? I was worried about you."

"Mama, you are going to be mad. I have something to tell you."

"What happened? I can see you were crying?"

"Oh, mama, there was this cake—a charlotte russe. It looked so delicious and I wanted it so badly. I didn't thing about the buns. When the salesgirl asked what I wanted, I just pointed to it. Then, I didn't have enough money to pay for the sweet rolls."

Handing the package to her mother, Adrianna fought back tears. "There are only six. I am so sorry, Mama."

Nonna took the package and held it in her hands, a puzzled expression in her eyes. "Only six? No, Adrianna, there are more than six in this package. Let's open it and see."

Nonna took a scissors from the kitchen drawer and snipped the red and white twine that encircled the white wax paper wrapped package. When the paper feel away, a dozen sweet rolls—no prune, no lemon, extra cheese—lay atop the table in all their sugary goodness. Adrianna's eyes opened wide.

"Mama, I ate the charlotte russe. I could only buy six buns."

"Well, *figlia mia*, the angels smiled on you today. Your good fortune does not excuse your thoughtlessness, but I hope you have learned your lesson. Sweets can become bitter very quickly when selfishness rules your heart and head. Sit down. Your father, sister and brother will want to hear your story. And while you wait for them, offer a prayer of thanks for the kindness you were shown. Someday you must repay that kindness by doing a good deed for another. And so that you don't forget, you will not eat any more sweets this week."

"Yes, Mama." Adrianna spoke her words with sincerity but her eyes told a different story. "I thought I would never eat a sweet roll or a charlotte russe again, but a week is a long enough punishment," they seemed to say.

***

Nonna was a wise woman and she did not believe in excessive punishment for children. She hoped that Adrianna's guilt would be punishment enough but as the years passed, she realized that a heavier hand might have been more effective in forming her daughter's character.

Whenever Palma heard the story of the charlotte russe, she wondered how Nonna had gotten so wise and why, since she was so wise, she had not been able to teach her daughter to love anyone but herself.

CHAPTER SIX

Whenever Palma was upset, she would call upon the memory of her grandmother and instantly feel calm.

"Nonna, I miss you so much."

With her estranged husband Jim coming for dinner, she needed to feel Nonna's hand resting firmly on her shoulder, providing much needed support... and she did. The wine also helped.
Palma was an excellent cook in her own right, but when preparing one of Nonna's recipes, she always faithfully followed the instructions as written.

Her grandmother's tightly joined, swirling script covered sheet after sheet of an old black and white composition book. Recipes cut from magazines and newspapers were glued haphazardly to some of the sheets, causing the pages to wrinkle. The uneven edges of the clipped recipes had turned brown with age reminding Palma of the liver spots on Nonna's hands.

There were no tabs in the composition book separating the selections into categories. No index of appetizers, entrees or desserts delineated the choices. Only the bent and torn corners, sooty grey from repeated turning with saliva moistened fingers, marked the oft prepared favorites.

Palma treasured the recipe book the way historians treasure the Dead Sea Scrolls. Although its grimy, dirt speckled cover was out of keeping with the modern chrome and wood trimmed décor, the book had a place of honor in the kitchen where it was displayed proudly on a weathered oak stand on the counter. The ink may have faded and the pages may have been soiled but to Palma, it was a priceless heirloom. No chef, real or imagined—

not Betty Crocker, Julia Child or Lidia Bastianich—could ever surpass Nonna in Palma's eyes. In case of fire, the recipe book would get saved first.

Each time Palma prepared a dish from the cherished notebook, especially the marinara sauce, she relived those carefree days when her grandmother's presence made home a happy place. She could not help but pretend to be that little girl again. Sauce simmering and ready for tasting, Palma whispered in her best imitation of Nonna, "Palma. *Venire. Mangi.*" Then, holding one hand under her chin, she licked the wooden spoon, rubbed her lips together and pursed her mouth. "It's so good, Nonna," she assured her grandmother.

Knowing that the evening's meal was important to her future happiness, Palma prepared dinner with extra care. The table, set for two, had been beautifully transformed from every day to special occasion. Gone were the woven bamboo mats that usually marked each setting. The chrome and glass table was covered with a white linen cloth bought especially for this night. Matching napkins, folded into fans graced the tablescape. White china etched in a silver filigree pattern formed a porcelain tier at each setting... salad plate atop dinner plate, crowned by a stemmed compote in which the appetizer would be served. Crystal goblets and her mother's wedding silverware sparkled in the reflected light from the low hanging ceiling fixture. Palma had polished each fork, knife and spoon until the utensils' rich, aged patinas shone brightly. A small bouquet of deep purple violets in the center of the table added the perfect finishing touch. Purple violets, silver and crystal—Palma stood back and admired her handiwork.

Reaching the decision to invite Jim to dinner had not been easy. Palma was threatened by him, fearful of being alone in his company. She doubted that much would be accomplished but hoped that her efforts at friendship would ease the way toward healing and encourage Jim to move on with his life. She had planned this dinner with only one thought in mind... freedom. To that end, she put extra care into the preparation of some of Jim's favorite foods.

The crab, lobster and shrimp appetizer in a spicy remoulade sauce was expensive to make but would show that she remembered and cared. A simple mixture of fresh greens—radicchio for bite, romaine from crunch and red leaf lettuce for color and sweetness—topped with sliced pears, golden raisins, walnuts, pignoli nuts and gorgonzola cheese would be the perfect second course. Lightly coated in a dressing made from equal parts sugar, apple cider vinegar and oil and seasoned with celery salt and pepper, it would both cleanse the palate and prepare it for the main course.

Normally, Palma served a separate pasta course and allowed a meat dish to complete the meal, but Jim, a creature of habit, had made it clear by throwing a dinner plate against the wall that he considered pasta to be the main course. The only meat he wanted were a few of Nonna's specialty meatballs, and he wanted them placed atop of his spaghetti just as his mother had done. To please his palate, a dozen of those tasty orbs were waiting to be warmed in the pot of sauce, but on this night the meatballs had one extra ingredient. Palma hoped its potent power would not fail her. When crushed, caster beans looked very much like pignoli nuts.

Although she had hinted at a reconciliation when she telephoned Jim with her dinner invitation, Palma's veiled hint had been a ploy. She had not wanted to trick him, feared his reaction if he realized her deceit, but she knew that he would not be able to resist the opportunity to gloat. Jim had been pursuing Palma relentlessly, insisting that she would crawl back to him one day. Leaving and returning had been a way of life for Palma during the first twelve months of marriage misery.

As a young newlywed, she'd been a sucker for Jim's tearful apologies and promises of change, but by the end of the first year she'd realized that Jim's promises were not worth the breath needed to speak them. It had taken a great deal of courage, a black eye and three broken ribs to push her past the breaking point. Regrettably, she had yet to find Jim's breaking point... the place at which he conceded that their marriage was over and nothing he did would change that.

Beginning early in their marriage, excessive drinking exacerbated Jim's already unbalanced state of mind, making rational thinking impossible. Why he thought she would allow herself to be abused again was a mystery. How he imagined that she could forget the mental abuse, beatings and death threats was even more mind boggling. Palma prayed that her efforts tonight would be rewarded. She needed Jim out of her life for good... for forever. To that end, the divorce papers lay waiting nearby for his signature. If he refused, only one option remained.

For the past two years, Palma had conceded to every demand Jim made in their divorce negotiations. Wanting to reach a settlement quickly, she had agreed to pay off all the debt he had accumulated during their marriage and after their separation. As a show of good faith, she had left behind everything except her clothing and toiletries when she moved out. Jim was left with a fully furnished apartment while Palma was forced to live with her mother—a situation not unlike that she had with Jim. With each concession, Jim had promised to sign the papers and then had quickly reneged. Tormenting Palma was his new favorite hobby.

Jim knew how to hurt Palma without leaving marks. He called her incessantly at work and at home. He stalked her at her place of business. He often showed up at social gatherings, leaving Palma to wonder how he knew where she would be.

When Palma decided to leave Jim, she had acted on the decision quickly. Throwing her clothes into boxes and bags, she had loaded her car and disappeared without a warning. In her haste, she forgot to pack her pajamas and nightgowns, which had been stored in the bombe chest on her side of the bed. Palma knew they were still there because Jim claimed to wear them whenever he "... needed to feel close..." to her. Palma's skin crawled at the memory.

Feeling the beginnings of another anxiety attack, the almost daily reminders of her days as Jim's wife, Palma took a deep breath. She needed to take control of her thoughts... to banish her fears. She reached for the glass of wine.

CHAPTER SEVEN

Happiness was not a word Palma associated with her child-hood. Neither was unhappiness. Resignation best described her feelings. When just a child she accepted that her life was misera-ble and would remain so for many years. Many hours had been spent resting her head against the bathroom towel bar; her face buried in the soft cloths to muffle her crying. "I hate her! I hate her! I wish I was dead!" Palma didn't really want to die. She just wanted to be somewhere else, anywhere else... far away from her mother.

Palma had been an infant when her grandmother moved into her parents' house. She was seven when Nonna died. The bond formed during those years was the lifeline Palma clung to when circumstances pushed her to the edge. Nonna holding Palma in her lap; Nonna rocking Palma in her arms; cooking and baking together; talking and praying together—the memory of her grandmother always lifted her up from despair. No matter how often she grappled that symbolic rope, her resolve never frayed or weakened.

The Rigo family—Adrianna, Joe, Palma and Nonna—lived on the top floor of a two story house. The carpeted staircase lead-ing to their apartment was steep and narrow. Because hip prob-lems prevented Nonna from climbing the stairs, making her a virtual prisoner in her own home, the front door was always left unlocked. Friends came to visit every morning.

"*Buon giorno*, Amalia," one friend after another called from the entry way.

"*Benvenuto*," Nonna called back.

Some of the women came alone. Often, they came in pairs. Always they brought something delicious from their kitchens. Palma had many favorites including pignoli cookies, anise biscuits and the dark, moist cakes flavored with espresso and sweet vermouth and enriched with dates, raisins and walnuts which were called fruitcakes but were nothing like the holiday paperweights of the same name.

After laboring up the steep steps, visitors were forced to pause for breath. Nonna, leaning on her ever present cane, would already be pouring the freshly brewed coffee and steamed milk in deep cups. Sitting nearby in her highchair, Palma would be cooing for attention, and each Zia, so dubbed by blood and friendship, would rush to pinch her cheeks and exclaim, "*Que bella.*"

In the afternoons, Nonna would sit in a chair by the living room window and hold Palma on her lap. She smiled and waved to the neighbors who would acknowledge her as they passed by. Raising Palma's little hands above the window sill, she would wiggle her fingers and encourage her to wave. "Wave *ciao* to Zia Maria, Palma. Wave to Zio Alex."

Nonna adhered to the customs of the old country where neighbors were more than friends. Everyone was family. When entering the United States, people chose to settle in areas where others of their ethnicity already resided. Italians with Italians. Germans with Germans. Irish with Irish. This was how every nationality kept its customs and traditions alive despite having left their homeland.

***

When Adrianna became an adult, she got a job as a mender and office manager in an embroidery factory. Her sister, Idalia, did the same. Confined for long hours each day inside a stuffy un-air conditioned building and deafened by the constant clatter of the huge machines as they punched decorative designs into bolts of cloth, the women grew more and more disillusioned with their lives. Both Adrianna and Idalia got married and both had families. Idalia found a way to turn her disappointment into some measure of happiness. She loved her husband and children.

Adrianna hated being a working mother. Actually, she mostly hated being a mother. She enjoyed the socialization and the feeling of importance that work provided. Arriving home each night, she would complain about the extra chores a baby created. Nonna seldom mentioned that she did most of them.

"I work all day long. I don't want to work when I get home. Joe wanted this child; he should take care of her. She will make me old before my time."

To emphasize her displeasure, Adrianna would slam cabinet doors and banging pots on the stove. Some nights, a sleeping Palma, startled by the commotion, would awaken and cry in terror. To calm Palma, Amalia would pick her up and cradle her close to her breasts. Resting her cheek on the top of Palma's little blonde head, she assured the baby, "Nonna is here. Nonna is here."

When Adrianna continued to complain, Amalia would sternly admonish her, "*Mio Dio*, Adrianna. *Basta! Basta!* Is it too much of a chore to hold your daughter and sing her a song?"

Adrianna would glare back at her mother but never offered her own daughter any affection. By the time Palma was three, she had grown too heavy for Amalia to lift onto her lap but she was not without protection. Amalia remained close by her side. When the yelling started, Amalia bundled the toddler into the soft, sagging fat of her arms and tucked Palma's head against her chest to ward off Adrianna's hurtful words.

Being maternal was not in Adrianna's nature. Much like when she was a child, she was too selfish to relinquish her place in the spotlight. She was jealous of the attention Palma received from family and friends. Her narcissistic temperament demanded that she be the center of attention. Each Valentine's Day she sent herself a bouquet of roses, claiming an anonymous admirer had left them at the door. For her birthday, a large box of chocolates arrived in like manner. No one was fooled, but no one dared voice the truth. Everyone played along, even Palma's father, admiring the flowers and sampling the candy.

"Only a broken hearted man," Joe patronized his wife, "would continue to pursue a woman—a beautiful woman—after she married."

Prisoners of circumstance, Amalia, Joe and Palma enjoyed the brief respite those self-deluding gifts provided. Briefly, Adrianna was happy but as each flower wilted and the candy box emptied, the fantasy faded away. An impressionable Palma grew to associate roses and chocolates with deception and subterfuge. She was never able to accept either as a gift no matter how sincere their intent.

Joe and Adrianna fought constantly over his insistence that they have a child. Motherhood did not fit in with Adrianna's vision of herself as a sexy, vivacious head turner. She feared the loss of her figure, which she emphasized with pushup bras and short, form fitting clothing. Despite her explosive commentary whenever the topic of more children arose, there was never any doubt that Joe would win the battle. As Catholics who followed the church's teachings against birth control, the outcome was predetermined. Joe was overjoyed when Adrianna became pregnant with Palma. Adrianna cursed him and their unborn baby. Her anger was the sword she used to slice away his happiness and self-respect.

Home became a war zone. The more obvious Adrianna's pregnancy, the more hostility she exhibited. Amalia and Joe resembled infantrymen under attack. The verbal bullets Adrianna shot at them were just as painful and destructive as artillery fire. Palma joined their ranks at birth. Adrianna refused to get up at night to feed the baby. She demanded that Joe change diapers whenever he was home from work. Amalia rocked her granddaughter to sleep when she was cranky. United against a common enemy, Joe and Amalia protected Palma from harm. Amalia also protected her son-in-law, whom she loved dearly. Like soldiers in battle, they were constantly on alert for incoming mortars.

Palma's well being was guaranteed while her grandmother was alive, but her death changed the balance of power. Adrianna then ruled exclusively. While she lived, Amalia stood strong against her daughter's hurtful actions. Since Adrianna felt she had married below her station, nothing Joe did was ever good enough and Adrianna reminded him of her disdain daily.

"I could have married money. I had so many boyfriends. I was crazy to choose you! Look what you come from… low life. No class!"

Years of browbeating demoralized Joe and took its toll on his health. Amalia's love for her son-in-law only made things worse.

"Adrianna, basta! Leave Joe alone. He is a good man. He works hard for you and the baby."

"Mama, do not tell me what to do. This is my house. Do you have somewhere else to live?"

Joe, knowing better than to argue, would pat his mother-in-law on the shoulder in gratitude. Although just a little girl, Palma sensed her father's shame. He rarely spoke up in defense of himself. When Amalia died, Palma not only lost her grandmother, she lost her father as well… at least, in spirit.

CHAPTER EIGHT

With the protective shield of her grandmother's presence gone, Palma was propelled into a world inhabited by mistreated stepchildren and abused orphans. She thought of the stories she had read and wished for a happy ending, but this diminutive Cinderella knew she had no hope of being rescued by a fairy godmother and talking mice. There would be no magic wand waved over her head, transforming her from unwanted child to adored daughter.

Palma's days were defined not by ashes and soot but by dust—dusty blinds, dusty tables, dust on the backs of the sofa and chairs... lots of dust... real and imagined. Her hands were raw from washing the toilet and tub; her knees cracked from scrubbing the floors. The contents of the rag bag were more familiar to her than the clothes hanging in her closet. The old discarded shirts and towels were kept on the stairway leading to the unheated attic. A blast of cold air in winter and a surge of suffocating heat in summer enveloped Palma whenever she opened the door. The only good thing about that bag was that it held a few of Nonna's housecoats, cut up for polish cloths. Seeing them always made Palma feel better. She would hold a piece of fabric to her nose and, even though the only thing she could smell was detergent, she imagined her grandmother and was able to smile.

As she grew older, Palma escaped into her fantasies. When she thought of her first year of life, before Nonna's arrival, she pictured an old 8mm camera spooling out a film one cell at a time.

Fade in: On the grainy negative, Adrianna would be seen soaking a cloth diapered Palma's backside in floor polish before sitting her on the linoleum. Smiling for the camera, her mother would then insert a broom handle into the back of Palma's diaper and begin to push her infant daughter around the kitchen, dragging her back and forth over the dirty floor. **Fade out**.

None of the neighbors were fooled by Adrianna's pretense as loving, caring wife and mother. Even with the windows closed, she could be heard yelling from blocks away. Palma's painful sobs were heard as well. Rarely did a day pass without punishment meted out for some imagined wrong. In truth, Palma was suffering for something she had no control over... being born.

***

The neighborhood of Palma's youth was more than a collection of houses lived in by strangers. The adults were all honorary aunts and uncles. They brought respect to those titles by offering Palma the affection she so desperately craved. Their memory never faded.

Aunt Marie and Uncle Carmen, Aunt Anne, Aunt Rita and Uncle Fred, Aunt Ellen and Uncle Bill... good people all. If not for the kindness of these extended families and the friendship of their children, Palma shivered to think what may have become of her. The invitations of these generous people—dinner, parties, ice cream, cookies, the drive in, car rides—brought joy to an otherwise dismal existence.

Katherine Maloney was Palma's best pal growing up. She was a petite, skinny, bespectacled girl who made up for her small frame with a fierce loyalty. Katherine lived five houses away and a world apart.

Mr. Maloney, Katherine's father, was a police officer. He was a stern, serious man who Palma greatly admired. Tall and imposing in his uniform, his holster and baton hanging securely around his waist, he filled Palma with absolute confidence that no criminal would escape his grasp. Occasionally, he took Katherine and Palma for a ride in his patrol car. How important they felt sitting in the back seat, straining their necks above the window frame in the hope that their friends would see them.

While Palma and Katherine stretched their necks to become taller, Officer Maloney was struggling in the reverse. No matter how low he adjusted his seat, his head brushed against the roof of the car, making Alfalfa-like cowlicks in his hair. Palma and Katherine would poke each other as a warning to stifle their giggles as the errant strands danced with static electricity.

Katherine's mother, Nancy, was a stay-at-home mom. She baked often and always had a treat waiting when the girls got home from school. Her kitchen smelled of cinnamon, ginger and nutmeg. Palma thought Mrs. Maloney's oatmeal cookies were better than anything made at the bakery. Of course, she confided to herself, they could never be as good as Nonna's, but Nonna was gone and homemade anything had become a rarity. As the sweet goodness of the cookies filled Palma's belly, the hole in her heart left by Nonna's death grew bigger.

Palma and Katherine were in the same class at St. Mary's Catholic Grammar School. Whether walking to or from school, lunchtime and recess, they spent every free moment together. In warm weather, they sat on Palma's front porch, schoolbooks spread out around them, and did their homework. In winter, they stayed warm in the Maloney kitchen, books spread out on the kitchen table.

Saturday was chore day, at least for Palma, and like a conjoined twin, Katherine was right there beside her. As the sun peaked over the horizon, the best friends would set off to do the Rigo family grocery shopping. Although as a child Adrianna had been an expert at spying bargains and directing her mother's purchases, she now detested going to the supermarket. She often boasted that her family was descended from royalty and royalty did not shop for themselves. Palma rolled her eyes each time her mother made the claim of high birth. When she reached her teens, she began to think the claim must be true. After all, her mother was "… a royal pain in the ass." Fearful that such sentiments would lead to more punishment, she kept her thoughts to herself.

Not until after Nonna's death was the claim of royal birth revealed by Adrianna. By then, Palma had been deemed old enough to handle the chores. She never understood how her mother could be regal but she, the daughter of the queen, be nothing but a lowly parlor maid. If the family was truly royalty, wouldn't that have made her a princess? When in the line of ascension, she wondered, did the claim to the throne pass solely to the queen mother, ignoring her husband and child? The Peasant Princess… that's how Palma saw herself, and she and Katherine shared many laughs over Palma's feigned air of noble mien.

Singing "A tisket, a tasket, pulling a metal basket," the two friends set off to perform their royal duty. With one hand each extended behind their backs, Palma and Katherine dragged the wire shopping cart as they trudged to the store. Summer and winter, rain or shine, every Saturday morning, Katherine stood waiting on the sidewalk outside Palma's house at 6:00 am. The hour was early for two young girls to be walking the streets, but Adrianna insisted that Palma be at the store when the doors opened… before the bins and shelves of freshly stocked produce were picked over by other customers. Adrianna was a grocery snob long before gourmet chefs became household names, a carryover from her childhood when friendships with the local merchants was something to be desired. She believed that the size and freshness of the fruits and vegetables she bought set her apart from other wives. The crispness of a head of lettuce, the size of an artichoke… these were the scales by which she weighed her superiority.

Each week's grocery list was Herculean, requiring Palma and Katherine to make three or four trips to the supermarket. All the clerks knew them by name. With big smiles, the cashiers and stock boys would greet their arrival.

"Good morning, Palma. Good morning, Katy, my girl," Brian,

the cart boy, would welcome them as he rolled the snaking line of baskets out to the curb.

"Not Katie. My name is Katherine. I tell you that every week, Brian." Katherine's pretense at being annoyed fooled no one. She enjoyed being teased by Brian, whose attention made both girls feel special.

"Katherine it will be from now on," Brian promised, but his memory was short lived. Each week as Palma and Katherine left the store, he would call out, "A fine day to you, Katy and Palma. Until next week…" Both girls offered a cheerful wave in return.

Brian was just one of the many people who took the time to assist the girls. As they were always sweet and polite, the sales staff were eager to help them make their purchases—counting out the money, making change and bagging groceries. The bags they could not carry were kept in a shopping cart near the door, watched over by the store manager until they returned for them.

For five years, the two best friends spent their Saturday mornings trekking back and forth to the Shop Rite. Brunette and blonde, short and tall, bespectacled and clear eyed, side-by-side, the girls were a familiar sight in the neighborhood. Then, shortly after Palma's twelfth birthday, everything changed.

The Maloney family moved away and Palma was on her own. She never saw Katherine again, but she never forgot her. Saturday morning shopping continued but now Palma was alone.
Brian's welcome – "Good morning, Palma, my girl." – no longer brought a smile to her face. She missed her friend almost as much as she missed Nonna.

Palma learned at a very young age that love and friendship brought pain. She began to wonder if, perhaps, it was better to go through life without either and for the next five years that is exactly what she did.

CHAPTER NINE

Once all the groceries had been carried home, unpacked and put away, the remainder of Palma's Saturdays was spent cleaning the house. She hated cleaning the venetian blinds most of all. There were 15 windows in the house, all covered with the dreaded metals slats. Dusting and washing them usually resulted in cut fingers. The blinds were decorated with a grey speckled pattern that made it difficult to see what was clean and what was dirty. Poised like a ballerina on pointe, Palma need to balance herself on the uppermost step of a ladder to reach the top of the window. She would gladly have made a deal with the devil to be spared this chore, not because she feared falling but because falling would have resulted in a beating from her mother.

"Palma, be sure to wipe the blinds on both sides. And don't get your fingerprints on the glass." Week after week, Adrianna's orders never varied.

Palma parroted her response so often—"Yes, mother. I'm being careful not to touch the window."— she felt it would be a fitting epitaph for her tombstone. Whatever task she was assigned, Palma made sure to do it perfectly. Not doing so would risk a beating. Adrianna checked on her progress by running a white-gloved finger over every dust collecting surface. Palma held her breath. The back of her head had felt the blow of her mother's hand too often to be ignored. Adrianna's aim was always accurate.

Beatings were as persistent as the dust. No matter how often Palma wiped dust from the furniture, there was always more dust to wipe away. The same was true for punishment. Hitting and kicking were common; biting was more rare but, along with pinching, her mother's attacks left a fair amount of bruising on

Palma's skinny arms and legs.

When really angry, Adrianna whipped Palma with a dog's heavy chain leash. The dog, a beautiful cocker spaniel named Taffy, was long gone. The welts left by the leash on Palma's back and shoulders were hidden under long-sleeved shirts and sweaters—pretty clothing to cover the ugliness of her life. The black and blue marks healed with time but as the discoloration on her skin faded from purple to green to yellow, Palma's spirit also faded. She no longer felt love or hate; her heart became an inhabitable wasteland except for the chamber where memories of Nonna, her father, Katherine and Taffy were kept hidden away.

Taffy, the furry little bundle of unconditional love, had been a Christmas gift from a kind relative who recognized the loneliness and despair in Palma's eyes. How excited she had felt sitting cross-legged on the living room floor while opening the big box that never stopped moving. Palma had wanted a puppy. She had dreamed of having a puppy and here was the perfect one—white and brown spotted with long floppy ears and a wet, scratchy tongue meant for washing away her tears. Palma loved Taffy on sight. As soon as she pulled open the box top, the puppy bounded into her arms. Together, they fell back onto the carpet. A strange sound escaped Palma's throat. It was laughter. The kind that could be felt down deep in her belly. The kind of laughter that lightened the weight on her soul.

While Taffy covered Palma's face with kisses and poked her nose inquisitively into Palma's ears, Adrianna fumed. She had hated the dog on sight. Another inconvenience—something more to complicate her life. Children and animals… she wanted neither in her home.

Palma did not understand how her mother could resist picking the puppy up and cuddling it in her arms. She was too young to see the correlation between her mother's refusal to hold the infant Palma with her lack of enthusiasm for the dog. Daring both her husband and her daughter to defy her, Adrianna insisted that Taffy be kept chained to the kitchen radiator when inside the house. The puppy's only freedom was when taken for a walk. All day long, it was confined to the small space under the corner writing desk.

Even when Palma was home from school, Taffy had to remain on the chain. The kneehole where the desk chair usually stood became both cell and playground; two gentle creatures caged without bars but nonetheless imprisoned.

Palma hated her mother's cruelty toward Taffy. Like her owner, the dog's only crime was living in a loveless house. Taffy grew to fear the sight of Adrianna. She showed her frustration by snapping at her each time Adrianna got too close. Palma understood the dog's anger. She, too, felt chained to the radiator with no hope of escape.

One Sunday while Palma was at mass, Taffy slipped out of her collar and charged Adrianna, who ran, screaming, into the bathroom. With the dog snarling at the door, she yelled out the window for her husband, who was trimming the hedges in the backyard. "Joe! Joe! Help! The dog has gone mad!"

If, indeed, it was madness, only one person was at fault. Taffy loved Palma and Joe. They had only to call the dog's name and, tail wagging, she would come running. Rolling onto her back, she waited eagerly for belly rubs. That is how Taffy was remanded to her cell under the desk... Joe whistled, the dog came running, rolled over and the "noose," as Palma called it, was slipped around her neck.

A week later, Taffy had a new home. Palma and Joe could no longer watch her suffer. They sat together, holding back tears, and discussed what was best for the dog. Joe placed an ad in the paper—*Housebroken puppy. Female. Friendly. AKC registered. Looking for loving family.* They got an immediate response.

Mr. and Mrs. Caso were thrilled to adopt Taffy. They thought she was beautiful and found her soulful eyes and happy disposition irresistible. Palma wished they had wanted a housebroken little girl as much as they wanted her dog. The leash was the only reminder that Taffy had ever belonged to her. If threatening to bite her mother would have set her free, Palma would gladly have sunk her teeth into her flesh.

CHAPTER TEN

There was no joy in the Rigo household. Holidays and birthdays were particularly dismal affairs. Palma's father was a loving man, and she knew he adored her, but he was incapable of protecting her from her mother's cruelty. He couldn't protect himself either. Joe was good. Adrianna was evil and evil was stronger. After so many years in an unhappy marriage, Joe was a dejected man whose life revolved around working, eating, sleeping and waiting to die.

Palma had witnessed her father's humiliation over and over again. She remembered some incidents more clearly than others. One, in particular, had exposed Joe's powerlessness and convinced Palma that nothing she could do would ever change their circumstances.

In the wee hours of morning, when only devils and demons were awake, Palma was roused from sleep by a commotion in the kitchen. Adrianna was loudly berating Joe for eating a banana before going to bed and leaving the peel in the garbage pail under the sink. Awakened at 3:00 am by his wife's condemnation of his thoughtlessness in leaving the offensive peel in the house, Joe stood barefoot in his pajamas while Adrianna ranted on and on. Claiming she could smell the banana's decaying odor, she waved the garbage bag in the air, hitting her husband in the back of the head. He had no option but to get dressed and take the bag out to the street. Not a word passed his lips, perhaps, fearing that if he verbalized his thoughts, self-control would be lost and the situation would escalate into violence he was not prepared to handle.

In her bedroom across the hall, Palma heard everything. She cautiously cracked open the door and peaked out. When, she wondered, had the father she knew ceased to exist. Joe had always been a gentle man; a soft-spoken man who never raised his voice or his hand in anger. He could be hard as stone when he needed to be but he was also soft as velvet when Palma needed support. He was a stranger to prejudice and racism. Those words did not even exist in his vocabulary. Although he had only a high school education, he was smart... very, very smart. There was no question he could not answer, no math problem he could not solve; no sentence he could not diagram. He was a story teller and a poet. Palma got her love of words and language from him.

In Palma's eyes, Joe was the wisest and kindest person in the world. He felt other people's pain deeply, especially his daughter's. If Palma stubbed her toe, Joe limped. If Palma sprained her wrist, Joe's hand ached. If Palma failed a test, Joe suffered the disappointment with her. When Adrianna's cruelty made Palma cry, Joe held her in his arms and cried with her. Palma looked up to him. She depended on him. But on this morning, she wondered where her daddy had gone. That could not be him standing so defeated in the kitchen. She loved him with all her heart, but her respect for him was slowing going the way of the banana peel.

Though the memory was hazy, Palma recalled going to the movies one Saturday—one Saturday only—with her father. A Disney film was playing at the local cinema. She did not remember which one. It really didn't matter. What was important was that she was with her father... and her mother was at home. Together, they sat in the dark sharing an armrest. Palma had her legs tucked under her so that she could see over the people in front. She remembered the feeling of serenity that had overcome her although, at the time, she could not have given that feeling a name. All she knew was that she had never felt that way before. For a few hours, father and daughter were able to shut out the world. Hand in hand, they walked the ten blocks home when the movie was over. Palma had silently wished it was ten thousand blocks. She wondered if her father felt the same way.

Whenever sorrow threatened to overtake her, Palma would reach back into the past for that memory. Two hands...

one large, one small… holding tightly to each other. Long strides shortened to match a little girl's slower pace. One Saturday. One happy memory.

Palma's only birthday party the year she turned eight was a fiasco. Her classmates, all girls, were gathered around the kitchen table. An ironing board had been placed across the chairs to make enough seating space. The celebration was going well until Carol Kane wet herself, urinating through her clothes and soaking the ironing board cover.

At first Carol said nothing, but when the girls sitting to either side of her felt their seats become damp, they jumped up in disgust. Carol began to cry. To be fair, she had been trapped against the kitchen wall between four other guests. Getting out would have meant pulling the table away and risking spilling the refreshments. Adrianna's fanatical need for neatness was well known. Carol, Palma never doubted, was more afraid of asking to leave the table then of embarrassing herself. Her classmates forgave her immediately.

Adrianna seethed. Furious with Carol, she hid her anger behind a fake smile and a "That's okay, dear," expression of concern. Like the perfect hostess, she helped Carol to remove her soiled garments and gave her a pair of Palma's pants to wear. As the girls played games, Adrianna removed the wet ironing board cover and padded the board with towels so that the party could continue. After everyone went home, her anger erupted. Palma was accused of intentionally giving Carol too much soda.

"Why did you keep filling her glass?"

"I didn't, mommy. She poured her own soda."

"You must have known she had to go to the bathroom."

"I didn't know. She didn't tell me."

"I saw the girls laughing."

"We were just having fun."

The sound of Adrianna's hand making contact with Palma's face was thunderous.

"Go to your room. I'll deal with you later."

The ridiculousness of accusing an eight-year- old of such a conspiracy eluded Adrianna. Palma knew there would never be another party. She knew not to wish for a happy birthday. Disappointment was all she ever got.

Christmas was a special kind of hell. Adrianna cared nothing about what her daughter might like as a gift. She paid for presents but never shopped for them herself. Instead, she gave money to one of Palma's aunts and asked her to "... buy Palma whatever you are buying for your kids."

Those kids were Peggy and Johnny... Palma's cousins. Palma was the oldest, then came Peggy and then Johnny. They were one year apart from each other. Aunt Edna, Peggy's and Johnny's mother, brought the gifts to the house during one of her visits and Adrianna would put them under the tree on Christmas Eve. The gifts were never wrapped.

Palma was allowed to play with the toys until New Year's Day. Then, so the house would always be neat, they were relegated to the unheated attic. If Palma wanted to play, into the attic she must go, dressed like a Sherpa, bundled up in a coat, hat and gloves. Playtime was alone time as none of Palma's friends were willing to risk getting frostbite.

On her ninth Christmas, Palma received a life-sized doll that walked when her hand was held. She hated it. Her heart had been set on the silver and turquoise six shooters and the black and turquoise holster that were displayed in Albee's Toy Store window. Palma had talked about them for months and could not walk past the store without pressing nose to the glass. "Dolls," she had said so often her mother accused her of being a broken record, "are for babies and I'm no baby." Palma wanted to be a cowgirl.

Feigning pleasure at the gift, Palma plotted her revenge. While Adrianna was watching, she played quietly with the doll, combing her hair and hosting tea parties. As soon as her mother was out of sight, off came the head. Palma felt like the Queen of Hearts in *Alice in Wonderland*. By pulling on the tousled locks and jamming her fingers under the neck, she managed to pry the doll's head free of its rubber torso. Throwing it on the floor, she would pretend to cry until Adrianna came back into the room.

"Mommy, the head came off. Can you fix it?"

"Palma, how did this happen?"

"I don't know, mommy. It just fell off."

When the toy store opened for business the next day, Adrianna and Palma would be waiting. The salesman inspected the doll and, finding no reason to doubt their story, replaced it with a brand new doll. Palma was miserable. She wanted those guns. Again, she waited patiently, playing with the unwanted gift whenever her mother was watching. When she wasn't... off came the head. Twice more the doll was replaced. Twice more it suffered the same fate. Adrianna never suspected that Palma was the culprit. Tired of the trips to the store, Adrianna stuffed the doll in the back of the closet never to be looked at again. Palma still wanted the guns and, finally, got them for her tenth birthday.

Christmas was always about outdoing the neighbors. Every year Adrianna insisted on buying the biggest tree that would fit into the living room. She never considered the difficulty of getting it through the narrow front door and up the steep staircase. That was Joe's job.

Immediately after Thanksgiving, Joe would begin to decorate the tree. He strung the lights and hung the ornaments. He put the tinsel on the branches one strand at a time, making sure the each piece was equidistant from the one next to it. Palma helped to hang the plastic icicles and had the honor of putting the angel on the top.

Whenever Palma thought of Christmas, she thought of that angel. Until she was too big to pick up, Joe lifted her in his arms and held her steady while she slipped the white and gold satin clad plastic doll onto the top branch. Then, he would plug in the lights, pour a glass of blackberry brandy for himself and a glass of apple juice for Palma, and they would sit on the floor together, the lights reflecting in their eyes.

For the short while it remained in the house, the labor of love that was the Christmas tree stood in front of the living room picture window. It was a source of pride for Joe, but as soon as the needles began to drop, out it went. Adrianna could not tolerate the mess.

Never was a holiday dinner eaten at home. Adrianna's sister, Idalia, always invited the family and thankfully so. The Montemurro clan was large and with so many people gathered around the table, Adrianna was forced to be on good behavior. Even so, her strict enforcement of proper etiquette always caused tension.

"Palma, put your napkin in your lap."

"Palma, wipe your mouth."

"Palma, don't reach for the salt. Ask for it."

The fact that Palma was just a child was lost on Adrianna. Each command was accompanied by a smack on the leg or hand. Palma ate with a fork or spoon and drank from a cup by the time she was a year old. Adrianna insisted. No utensil... no food.

With Adrianna out of earshot, Palma's Aunt Idalia liked to tell the story of one particular Thanksgiving dinner. Since she was only 18 months old when this happened, Palma didn't remember the event, and even though she knew her aunt was being a little bit malicious, she couldn't help but smile.

After everyone had finished eating, Uncle Rocco, Idalia's husband, stood Palma on the dining room table. Staring hard at

Adrianna, he advised her to hold her tongue. Then, he allowed his little niece to walk across the table, stepping into the mashed potatoes and string beans along the way. To hear tell, the expression on Adrianna's face rivaled the gargoyles on Notre Dame. With a huff and a snarl, she scooped Palma up in her arms and left the room, but she never said a word to Rocco. He was more than a match for her.

Palma's Uncle Rocco had been a short but powerfully built man. His only obvious imperfection was a limp—the result of a birth defect. A difficult delivery had left him with one hip higher than the other and corrective surgery was not an option. The limp did not diminish his stature in the eyes of his family and co-workers. Palma adored him.

Rocco worked as a surveyor for a sand and gravel company. Although strong, it wasn't his physical presence that held Adrianna in check. The power of his mind was much more intimidating. Rocco was intelligent, conversant and well read. The bookshelves in the living room were filled with the words of great authors; the softened bindings and dog-eared pages a testament to the many hours spent engrossed in the stories. In a battle of wits and words, Rocco reigned supreme. No amount of yelling ever cowed him. He disapproved of Adrianna, and she knew better than to bait him. Seeing his own children and Palma happy were what mattered most. He loved his niece and did all he could to make her life less traumatic.

Sitting in Uncle Rocco's lap, in the big armchair next to the fireplace, Palma would snuggle against his chest while he read to her. Romeo and Juliet. Macbeth. A Yankee in King Arthur's Court. Palma may not have understood the words she heard but she did sense how important the stories were to her uncle. An excellent teacher by example, Palma always credited Rocco for her love of books.

CHAPTER ELEVEN

If salvation comes in human form, Palma's relatives were its incarnation. Her aunts, in particular, provided stability and asylum during those turbulent years. However, as Palma grew older, she grew more anxious and pensive.

"When I am 18…"

"When I graduate high school…"

"When I am older, I will escape," she promised herself.

At the age of 10, Palma began running away from home almost every Friday afternoon. She wasn't actually running away. She was running toward.

The school dismissal bell signaled freedom. Other students heard only clang, clang, clang as Sister Agnes Claire swung the bronze bell up and down. Palma heard, "Run, Palma, run."

Before Adrianna arrived home from work, Palma would pack her tattered red suitcase and hustle off to Aunt Idalia's and Uncle Rocco's house. The 90-minute walk was effortless. Mile after mile, block after block, whether traversing snow drifts or leapfrogging puddles, there was a playful lope to Palma's unhurried gait. The farther from home she got, the less weighty the burden she carried on her young shoulders. She knew that when she arrived at her aunt's front door, she would be welcomed with open arms and a hot meal.

After the initial scare of finding Palma gone, Joe knew not to worry. Once home from work, he would call Idalia to inquire about Palma's safe arrival. Although Adrianna always got home from work before her husband, she never called her sister. In fact, she rejoiced in Palma's absence and, if she came home to find Palma there, the weekend became a sequence of beatings and punishments. Against their better judgment, on Sunday evenings, amidst tears and protests, Idalia and Rocco brought Palma back home.

Aunt Idalia and Aunt Helen, the aunt who bought the Christmas presents, were Palma's guardian angels. Every spring, Idalia took Palma to Radio City Music Hall to see the Easter Show. Comfortably seated on a well-padded bench at the front of the bus, Palma would stare out the windshield during the hour's ride from New Jersey to 42nd Street in Manhattan. From there, Idalia would hail a cab to the theater. The bus and the taxi were Palma's windows to the world.

Waiting on the ticket line that coiled endlessly around the building, Palma could barely contain her excitement. She held tightly to her aunt's hand not wanting to be displaced by the ever growing throng of families and school groups. Once inside the theater with its red carpeted floors and gilded trim, Palma's eyes would become saucer shaped with happiness. She would twirl around and around like a music box ballerina, consigning all that she saw to the memory box in her mind.

As the band began to play and the curtain rose, a hoofer was born. The dazzling costumes and intricate routines... the music and the sound of the jingle taps against the hardwood floor... every sensory sensation filled Palma with excitement. Sliding to the edge of her seat, she craned her neck so as not to miss a single turn, strut or bow. Unselfconsciously, she pulsated with the beat. The Rockettes, arms linked and legs high kicking in unison, filled her with magical delight.

Back home, behind closed doors, Palma practiced time steps before the full length mirror that stood in the corner of her bedroom. Although she tried hard to keep a Broadway smile pasted on her face, she often scowled at the ineptness of her attempts. Feathers, pulled from the feather duster (when Adrianna wasn't looking) and pinned to her school beret became the fancy head dress the Rockettes wore. Only when Adrianna yelled, "Palma, stop stomping!" did she collapse on the floor, rolling onto her back to stare up at the ceiling. She didn't need to move her feet to dream.

On Saturday afternoons, Aunt Idalia and Palma often walked to Bergenline Avenue, the town's main shopping district. When the shopping was done, Idalia always bought them lunch at the local diner. No matter how many hamburgers Palma had eaten since her childhood, those greasy mounds, which were served with potato chips instead of fries, were the best. As she was not allowed snacks at home, the salty side dish was an extra special treat. Those lunches were also the only opportunity she had to put condiments on her food. Since Adrianna did not use mustard, mayonnaise or ketchup, Palma and Joe were not permitted to use them either.

Aunt Helen was a widow whose life revolved around her children. She loved Palma with the same deep affection that she showered on her own kids, and Palma had an open invitation to visit whenever she wanted. Had she lived closer—within walking distance—Palma would have run away to her house on alternate weekends.

In Aunt Helen's house there were no rules that could not be broken. She truly wanted kids to be happy and, as long as no one got hurt, she was content. Peggy, Johnny and Palma had only to mention what they wanted to do and Aunt Helen provided the means. With shaving cream, towels, combs, brushes and bladeless razors, the living room became a barber shop. PJ&P Restaurant opened with borrowed pots and pans, dishes, utensils and, of course, snack food. The entry hall made an excellent bowling alley when not being used as a roller skating rink.

Usually, Aunt Helen, Peggy and Johnny would visit Adrianna and Joe one Sunday a month. For some reason, Adrianna never felt ashamed of the unflattering differences in their parenting styles. The visit always began pleasantly but always ended poorly. Adrianna's anger over some imagined infraction developed into a hurricane of curses and cruelty.

Yelling led to hitting Palma with whatever was handy—her hand, a shoe, a wooden spoon, a belt. Face crumbling in tears and embarrassment, Palma would run to her room and hide. By then Peggy and Johnny were crying, too, in sympathy and fear.

Although Aunt Helen tried to intercede, nothing anyone said could change Adrianna's behavior. When Palma was in her teens, Aunt Helen confided that whenever Peggy or Johnny had misbehaved, removing a wooden spoon from a drawer and laying it on the kitchen table had been all the deterrent needed.

CHAPTER TWELVE

Adrianna never involved herself in anything that did not beam a positive spotlight in her direction. She never attended school functions. No school plays, teacher conferences or graduation ceremonies ever interrupted her self-reflection. She did not attend Palma's first communion or confirmation. Any event that did not have her as the center of attention was an excuse for becoming "deathly" ill. Her medical history was dramatic but inconsistent. Her symptoms, which only manifested when other people were present and she was being observed, seemed to miraculously disappear when alone. Despite being at death's door on numerous occasions, she was reluctant to go to the doctor, claiming, "There isn't anything they can do for me. God will decide." Other than regularly recurring migraines, Adrianna seemed prone to obscure diseases which only responded to people jumping and fetching at her beg and call.

Munchhausen's Disease, a fictitious disorder in which a person repeatedly and deliberately acts as if they have a physical illness when, in fact, they are perfectly healthy, is considered to be rare and was practically unheard of when Adrianna was a young woman. However, even without a formal diagnosis, her behavior indicated a classic case with all the text book signs being clearly evident.

After years of colds, viruses, hints of cancer, gall bladder issues, hernias and numerous falls, cuts and bruises – all self inflected – Palma was convinced that her mother had only to imagine being sick or injured and a malady/emergency would appear. Some of her favorites tricks were to drink sour milk, overdose on laxatives and burn herself while cooking. Whenever attention was in short supply, Adrianna would "forget" to take her blood pressure medicine.

Special occasions that required formal attire were attended wearing ace bandages that covered Adrianna's arms from wrists to elbows. The reason... crippling arthritis. A bottle of aspirin or prescription Fiorcet was ever present at her dinner plate...
migraines. Sometimes there was a cane or, at least, a limp from a sprained ankle. There were so many band aids on Adrianna's hands and fingers, she appeared to be wearing flesh colored gloves. To hear her tell it, those wounds were always caused by "accidentally" stitching herself to whatever garment she was mending on the sewing machine. Adrianna considered any wedding or funeral that did not result in her getting more attention than the bride and groom or corpse to be a failure.

Dining in restaurants was particularly trying. No sooner would the family be seated around the table than Adrianna would order a cup of tea, which she held against her forehead to soothe a sudden headache. Expressions of concern quickly dominated the conversation, making everyone else uncomfortable for feeling well. Timing the exacerbation of her symptoms to the delivery of the food, Adrianna would express her need to go home "immediately" in a quivering voice that could not be ignored. Since she did not drive (although she had a license), someone had to be inconvenienced to transport her back to her house. This meant that the driver had to leave his or her dinner to get cold and inedible. In the rare instance that Adrianna made it through a meal, she picked at her selection, pushing it around on her plate and claiming that she had little appetite. The portion was either too hot, too cold, too large or too small. Without failure, the food just wasn't as good as she could make it and more often than not "something" would give her a queasy stomach.

Every dinner out, whether in a restaurant or someone's home, included an obvious inspection of the silverware and glassware. Forks and knives were closely examined and rubbed with a napkin to wipe away non-existent food particles. Wine and water glasses were also polished with a napkin after being held up to the light. No matter how spotless the place settings, nothing ever met Adrianna's rigorous standards. Feigning disgust, she would refuse to eat until the offending items were replaced. Even then, she would sport an air of defeat at having to sacrifice her standards for less than ideal quality.

When Palma entered the third grade, she was given a key to the house. She wore the key on a long shoelace around her neck that was just loose enough to slip over her head. The term "latch key kid" had not yet become the catch phrase for a generation of children coming home to empty houses, but Palma epitomized its meaning. School was two and a half blocks away. During the lunch break, Palma was expected to walk home and begin preparations for dinner. She would eat a banana or peanut butter sandwich while peeling potatoes and setting the table. Not wanting to suffer the same fate as her father, she always remembered to take the banana peel with her when she returned to school, disposing of it in the lunchroom trash. After school, chores came first and had to be completed before starting her homework. Play time... there was very little of that.

Until Palma went to high school, Adrianna demanded that she be in the house by 7:00 pm and in bed by 8:00 every night even during summer vacation. The earlier Palma went to sleep, the sooner Adrianna could relinquish her minimal parental responsibilities. Seven o'clock sharp, Joe would whistle out the living room window—the signal to come home. Embarrassed and disgruntled, Palma would leave her friends to their fun-filled exploits.

This was the neighborhood Nonna had bequeathed to Palma. Insular and protective of its children, the streets afforded a safe place for kids to grow up. Boys and girls, teens and tots, laughed and played together. Danger was never an issue. Bike riders and roller skaters shared the sidewalks, while stick ball bases and hop scotch squares were chalked on the tarred roadway. Cries of "You're it!" and "One. Two. Three. Red light!" filled the after dinner hours. On hot summer nights, Palma would lie in her bed with the window open, listening to her playmates excited voices. Most nights she cried herself to sleep.

CHAPTER THIRTEEN

Due to Adrianna's violent temper, Palma's parents had few friends. One pseudo aunt and uncle as well as Joe's brother and his wife were the only people brave enough to socialize on a regular basis. Card playing was their recreation of choice.

Adrianna was a very poor loser. Games always ended in the most theatrical of ways—usually with Adrianna throwing the deck of cards at Joe's head and accusing him of cheating. A shower of aces, kings, queens and jacks rained down on the table. While Adrianna screamed vile epithets, Joe would attempt to reason with her.

"It's only a game, Audrey." Using Adrianna's nickname often had a calming effect. "You can't win every game, and I am not going to lose just to make you happy. Play without me from now on."

Joe stood firm for a week or two but eventually relented and the scene was repeated like an old phonograph stylus caught in the groove of a scratched 78 rpm record. Years later, Joe actually followed through on his threat. In exasperation, he gathered up the cards from the floor, opened the kitchen window, and pitched them into the dark street below. Game over.

Whenever company visited, Palma stayed in her bedroom listening to the radio or reading. She preferred to be where her mother could neither see her nor reach her. One evening, Joe knocked on the bedroom door and asked permission to sit with her for a while. Palma, of course, welcomed him in, but her easy assent belied her concern. Failing to hide the pained expression on his face, her father explained that Adrianna's foul language had shamed him in front of their guests. Too civil to shout back and never for a minute considering a physical reply, Joe took refuse with his daughter.

Throughout her life, Palma watched her father bear the abuse meted out by her mother with dignity. However, the more Palma witnessed his humiliation, the less respect she had for him. Raised Catholic, Joe never considered divorce, longing instead for the release that death would provide. He often would mutter to himself, "Maybe I won't be here tomorrow."

Uttered with the reverence of a prayer, Joe longed for the eternal sleep knowing it was his only escape. Palma imagined his ascension to the Pearly Gates as a dance routine. She suspected that when death finally released him from his earthly hell, Joe would "shuffle off to Buffalo" with a big smile on his face. She envisioned him wearing a top hat and tails, dancing like Fred Astaire up, up, up until he disappeared into the clouds. She was pretty certain he would be singing, "I'm free! I'm free! Look at me, I'm finally free."

Palma and her parents were actors in their own reality show long before reality shows were a reality. She lost count of the number of times a pot or pan was thrown across the kitchen like a fastball at the World Series. Adrianna's throwing arm could rival the pros. After being hit repeatedly, Joe became an expert at recognizing the signs. Without a mitt, he rivaled Johnny Bench behind the plate... the dinner plate.

When Palma was a little girl, she could not understand why her mother used her father for target practice. She never knew what small word or gesture would trigger Adrianna's outbursts. As she got older, she realized that the mere salting of food before it was tasted was reason enough for attack. Daring to use ketchup, mayonnaise or mustard was a major offense. Just a dollop of a condiment on anything other than a hamburger guaranteed 57 varieties of pain. Sugar bowls, glasses, pots, salt and pepper shakers... anything and everything was a possible weapon. The kitchen often resembled a missile range.

Imagined insults were most often the reason Palma was

banished during meals. She considered herself lucky the few times her mother merely pointed a finger toward her bedroom and ordered, "Go!" More often, punishment was physical. One of Adrianna's favorite tortures, at least until Palma turned 13, was to grab her daughter by her braids and lift her up until her feet dangled above the floor. Thirteen was when Adrianna finally relented and allowed Palma to get her hair cut. Up to that point, the braids hung below her waist and provided Adrianna with another way to inflict pain.

Getting into a fight with Adrianna while she was cooking added an extra element of suspense. Sharp knives waved mere inches from her nose made effective exclamation points. Palma was always surprised when her mother stopped short of drawing blood. The threat was real. Only once did she make the mistake of ignoring Adrianna's preference for physical violence and her shoulder still bore the faint imprint of her mother's teeth.

CHAPTER FOURTEEN

Attending high school provided Palma with little respite from the misery of her life at home. Occasionally, Adrianna would allow her daughter to attend a basketball or football game, but curfew was ridiculously early—barely more than the 7:00 pm of her pre-teen years. More often than not, she would give Palma permission to stay out late and then forbid her to go to the game at the last minute. Dangle the carrot. Pull it away.

By senior year, Palma was miserably unhappy. She was petrified of her mother and wanted only to be free to live life on her own terms. Rather than reveling in the excitement of graduation plans and parties, she anticipated a year exactly like the three previous years. No dances. No dates. Few friends and more of her mother's obscure reasons for punishment. However, what Palma anticipated and what destiny had in store for her were two drastically different outcomes.

Palma came face to face with her future at the Christmas dance, a much anticipated event almost as important as senior prom. Although expecting to be disappointed, she asked her mother for permission to attend. To her surprise and elation, Adrianna assented. Years later, Palma contemplated the adage "Be careful what you wish for" and realized the truth in those words.

Adrianna's sudden change of heart was a mystery to Palma— one she would never solve. Perhaps, fate or whatever one chooses to call life's director has a dark and evil sense of humor. Regardless of the reason, from that day forward Palma would wish that her mother had remained true to her character.

The school gymnasium swirled in a kaleidoscope of green and

red, silver and gold. An eight foot tree dominated one side of the cavernous room. The usually bare walls were hung with holiday banners and the much polished hard wood floor reflected the gaily colored lights hanging from the ceiling. Gone were the school uniforms. Gone as well were the usual tee shirts and jeans that marked the end of the school day. Throughout the county, a jumble of plaid skirts, khaki pants, levis and sneakers were piled in heaps on bedroom floors. Transformed, even if only for a few hours, the girls in fancy dresses and boys in rarely worn jackets and ties, played at being grown up. It was all illusion and in the morning the teenagers' faux sophistication would be sucked down the shower drain along with makeup and hair gel.

From across the room, Palma spied two boys in deep conversation near the DJ booth. With furtive glances, they looked her way until shoving each other in a "you go first" fashion, they strutted toward her with ill concealed nervousness. One of the boys Palma had known since grammar school; the other she desperately wanted to know. Tall and lean with dark, wavy hair and startling blue eyes, Jim McDonald was the "man" of her dreams.

"Hey." Keith, the grammar school chum, sidled up beside Palma. "This is my buddy, Jim. He's in my English class and wanted to meet you."

"Hi, Jim." Palma was nearly struck mute by Jim's good looks.

"Hey, Palma. Keith tells me you're a good dancer. Would you like to dance with me?"

"Keith's also a good liar. This is the first dance I've ever attended so he has no way of knowing just how many toes I've broken."

"I'll risk it." Jim put out his hand.

Displaying a confidence she did not feel, Palma placed her hand in Jim's and silently followed him onto the floor. Witty banter ran wild in her head but remained unformed as her tongue became glued to her teeth. "Say something," she admonished herself but the words just seemed to catch in her throat.

Palma and Jim danced to the music ricocheting off the gymnasium walls. At first, Palma kept her eyes on the floor to hide her nervousness. Jim was not discouraged. He bent low from his six foot three inch frame and closed the distance to Palma's ear so that his voice could be heard above the music. The next thing Palma knew they were comfortably discussing school and shared interests; their bodies getting closer and closer in order to be heard without shouting. When a particularly loud song was played, Jim teased Palma saying that they would need to learn sign language just so they could talk to each other. Palma laughed—the first real laughs of her life—and moved easily into his arms.

In the few minutes it took to spin a record, Palma lost her heart. She was crazy about Jim, who seemed to be all that she was not and wanted to be... self-assured, confident and a bit of a rebel. He had an Irishman's gift for gab, spinning tales of fun and freedom. When the evening ended, Palma prepared to say goodbye. Jim lived in the south end of the county whereas Palma lived to the north. Since he did not have a car, his trip home would require an hour's bus ride provided he was lucky enough to catch the last bus of the night. Otherwise, it was going to be a long, long walk.

Palma doubted they would ever see each other again. They may have attended the same school, but that school was co-institutional. Boys and girls did not have classes together or eat in the cafeteria at the same time. The only shared space was the library, ruled with a lemon sucking scowl by Warden Sister Margaret Mary and her yardstick. No prison was better guarded than St. Joseph's of the Palisades Catholic High School.

To Palma's delight, Jim offered to walk her home. Covering the distance would take at least a half hour and would cause Jim to miss his bus. He shrugged his unconcern.

"I don't mind walking. It's a nice night."

Donna M. Carbone

Palma struggled to hide her excitement. The December night was cold but neither she nor Jim felt chilled. Warmed by the heady rush of first love, two previously lonely people braved the darkness. Arms linked, they walked into the future—a future they did not yet realize had begun under the electronic score board covered with pine boughs and holly.

As January, February and March rushed by, Palma fell more deeply in love. By April, she had lost all reason. So over-whelmed was she by the intensity of her feelings, she began de-fying Adrianna's orders. She stopped asking for permission to attend school functions. On the weekends, she and Jim spent many hours in Greenwich Village and mid-town Manhattan just walking and enjoying their time together. Palma felt paroled.

More frequent became the moments when Palma would look at Jim from across a room and cry tears of happiness. There was nothing she wouldn't do for him. A spell had been cast and she could not—did not—want to wake up. By the end of their first year together, Palma saw Jim as her "happily ever after" man. He gave her the courage to stand up for herself against her mother's constant barrage of negativity.

In those early days of their relationship, there were lots of good times. Palma and Jim went to concerts at the Fillmore East and the Bitter End. The Fillmore was well-known rock promoter Bill Graham's music venue located in the Lower East Side near Second Avenue and Sixth Street. The stage played host to some of the biggest names in rock music—Jimmy Hendrix, the Allman Brothers, Sly and the Family Stone, the Grateful Dead, Jefferson Airplane. Although the list of notables was long and memorable at the Fillmore, Palma preferred the more low-key coffee house atmosphere at the Bitter End, where folk music and comedians reigned supreme.

In the mid-1970s, the club became a birthing room for legacy producing singers like Bob Dylan, Joni Mitchell, and Joan Baez. One of Palma's favorite memories was of seeing a young, hand-some rock and roller named Rick Nelson perform.

Nelson was the son of popular band leader Ozzie Nelson and his songstress wife, Harriet Hilliard Nelson. Like most Americans, Palma had grown up watching the Adventures of Ozzie and Harriet on television. The sitcom featured Rick and his older brother David as well as their parents. Palma vividly remembered standing in the crowd outside the theatre watching David interact with the fans like a true showman. He had been wearing a wrinkled seersucker suit—a strange memory which seemed never to fade.

Palma also remembered seeing the very popular David Steinberg do his standup routine. At the time, Steinberg was the number one comedian in the country and had the distinction of being the youngest person to ever guest host The Johnny Carson Show. There was one joke that Palma faintly recalled... a hazy memory of deep laughter having to do with a carrot and a donut walking down the street. With the passing years, Steinberg became a big name in Hollywood not so much for his standup but for his writing and directing. He had lots of awards under his belt and Palma still liked and admired him.

Whenever Palma and Jim spent the day in the Village, they would eat dinner at their favorite little hole-in-the-wall restaurant called the Mexican Village. Palma was addicted to the tamales which were handmade and reminded her of the polenta Nonna had cooked when she was a child. One of Palma's most cherished memories was seeing Elvis Presley in person at Madison Square Garden during his first New York concert in 20 years. The night was memorable on so many levels. Seeing the handsome and talented King with her own eyes left a permanent imprint on Palma's memory. Then, there was the stage show... the costumes, the music, the songs, the voice. Finally, there was the spectacle of a young woman leaping over the balustrade on the third level and diving to the stage below. The jump resulted in the fan sustaining two broken legs. While the audience gasped, the police swarmed the stage, reaching it before the lady even landed, and Presley never missed a note of the song he was singing.

Looking back, Palma admitted to herself that there had a been some good times. Those memories were all the more reason why her disappointment was immeasurable when Lancelot was revealed to be the Black Knight. By the time the façade fell away, Palma had lost her soul as well as her heart to Jim. Slowly, he whittled away what little self-confidence she had gained. He was a master manipulator. His once bright shining armor grew more tarnished by the day but Palma was unable to break free.

While in high school, Jim's sweet demeanor was nectar for an affection-starved Palma. Years later, she referred to that first year as his larvae stage. He treated her kindly. He always complimented her and took her side against her mother, actually fighting with Adrianna when she became abusive… something Joe had never done. Jim was fearless. He encouraged Palma to defend herself and constantly fed her desire to get away from home. His confidence made Palma strong. A diploma and an engagement ring symbolized the beginning of a new life. To Palma, the tiny diamond was the Rock of Gibraltar.

CHAPTER FIFTEEN

The minute Palma graduated high school, Adrianna enrolled her in a very prestigious two year business college. The reason for her largesse was not a softening of her hard heart but rather a tightening of the purse strings. No longer would Palma live at home for free. She was now expected to pay rent for her bedroom and contribute to household expenses. Adrianna knew that the better the job Palma secured, the more money she could demand in rent.

With degree in hand, Palma was immediately hired by a very well-known household cleaning products manufacturer on Park Avenue. For the next four years, her salary went toward room and board for both herself and Jim. Now in college on a partial scholarship, Jim was unable to afford housing, tuition, books, clothing, food and incidentals. His parents lived from paycheck to paycheck and so the burden to pay for his education fell on Palma's shoulders. Although she lived with her parents, Palma saw Jim's apartment as her home away from home and, since she was paying for everything, she spent as much time there as possible.

Jim may have been the one attending college classes, but Palma was getting an education of a sort as well. Many of the nights Jim did not go to class were spent slumming in Manhattan bars where, he claimed, he was networking for their future. Palma eventually began to recognize the names of his business associates—Johnny Walker, Jim Bean and Jose Cuervo. While Palma worked her life away, Jim partied and drank to excess. While he never expressed one word of appreciation for her efforts, he did manage to portray himself as a victim if she dared to utter one word of complaint about his non-existent work ethnic or his evening exploits.

Jim became a chameleon whose only purpose it seemed was to keep Palma off balance with his shifts in personality. One minute he was unbelievably kind, and the next minute he was unbelievably horrid. It was impossible to anticipate which Jim would appear so swift where the changes in his demeanor.

Not wanting to alienate his daughter, Joe was cautious about expressing his unease with the relationship. Instinct told him that Jim was not who he pretended to be, but there was nothing concrete to base his feelings upon. Only after carefully considering the possible fallout did he confide his fears to Palma.

"There's something about him, Palma. I'm damned if I say anything and damned if I don't. Please. Be careful."

Dismissing her father's concern for her well being, Palma proceeded with the wedding plans. The date was set for October 25th. The church had been reserved and the catering hall booked. Although Joe's words had sounded an alarm, Palma ignored the warnings. She would not allow her own disquieting thoughts to plant any seeds of doubt.

A month shy of their wedding, Jim drugged Palma. Premarital sex was not an issue; Palma had willingly given in to Jim's persistent arguments that "... love makes it right." She had agreed, with some reservations, to oral sex as she knew it pleased him. To Palma, oral sex was foreplay not the end game. She openly expressed her aversion to being the recipient of Jim's seed, but Jim continually insisted that she "Get over it." He was becoming increasingly insensitive to Palma's feelings and more aggressive in achieving his desired release.

Palma and Jim spent a beautiful Saturday in late September decorating their newly rented apartment. Jim surprised Palma with a specially prepared picnic style lunch. Throwing a blanket on the parquet floors, he arranged two small pillows for her to lean on. Onto the middle of the blanket, he ceremoniously placed a wicker basket which, when opened, revealed Palma's favorite cold meal—pasta primavera with shrimp and asparagus in a balsamic dressing. The aroma of fresh Italian bread made their stomachs growl.

With great flourish, Jim uncorked a bottle of cheap Merlot and poured some into the two plastic glasses strapped onto the cover of the basket. Leaning down to hand Palma her glass, he sloshed the crimson liquid over the rim and onto the blanket. Apologizing, he took the glass into the kitchen to wipe it clean.

Cleopatraesque, Palma reclined against the pillows and ate her meal. Sips of the now tainted wine followed forkfuls of pasta and bites of bread. The nameless drug that had been added during Jim's planned excursion to the kitchen was slowly taking effect. By her second glass, Palma began to feel disoriented. Initially thinking she was drunk, she laughed at her inability to hold her liquor. As she became weaker and her words became more slurred, fear replaced humor. Unable to lift her arms and legs, Palma was overcome with fear. She knew with certainty what Jim had done but was unable to defend herself.

Palma imagined herself as two people—the Palma on the blanket and the Palma floating above her, watching and waiting. The watching Palma was filled with terror and entreated Jim to protect her, but her words were soundless. She floated, helpless, as the Palma below, pinioned to the blanket by inertia, became the unwilling recipient of Jim's ministrations. Hours later, when the two Palmas were reunited, she confronted Jim with his betrayal and wept in confusion and anger.

"Why did you do that to me? How can you say you love me?"

Jim's laughing response scarred Palma's heart. "Come on. It wasn't so bad. I wouldn't have let you get hurt and now you know you won't die from swallowing."

Shame and hopelessness overtook Palma and prevented her from discussing the incident further. Jim still represented the lesser of two evils. She could not bear the thought of returning to her mother's house. Marriage was the only way out.

The lovely little apartment where Palma was violated became

the first in a succession of leases that were broken in the dead of night. Eight months after moving in, with Jim still not working or contributing to expenses, Palma was forced to pack their bags, rent a U-Haul, and creep away like the thief she felt herself to be. Each time they signed a new lease, Palma saw the pen as a shovel and the lease as her grave. All her dreams were crumbling like stale bread. Her life was unraveling. The location of the buildings went from good to bad to not much better than a slum. To Palma, the apartments represented the deterioration of her life.

October 25th dawned a perfect autumn day. Despite a strong belief that Palma was making a huge mistake, Joe walked her down the aisle. As he lifted her veil, he sought her eyes and promised, "When you want to come home, the door is always open." Unfortunately, he had failed to get permission from Adrianna before offering Palma a haven in the storm that was brewing.

Sitting side by side on the altar, Palma was unable to lift her head to look at Jim or their guests during the ceremony. Doubt, not shyness, kept her eyes focused on the floor. She was a coward and as such she prayed that, when the priest asked "Does anyone know a reason why this couple should not be joined in Holy Matrimony," someone would say, "I do!" But no one did and Palma lacked the courage to speak for herself. As she watched the wax drip from the lighted candles, Palma envisioned herself growing smaller and smaller until, pinched between two fingers, the flame of life was extinguished forever.

CHAPTER SIXTEEN

The wedding reception was held in a very popular Italian restaurant. Perhaps, things would have gone more smoothly if corned beef and cabbage had been on the menu. The obvious dislike of Jim's Irish relatives for Palma's Italian family kept conversations muted. All attempts at cordiality were rejected. An invisible curtain divided the room and effectively relayed the message to "Keep out!"

At Jim's insistence, no friends were invited. Palma had few anyway and none that Jim liked. In the five years they had been together, she could not remember socializing with anyone other than his siblings. The only party to which they had ever been invited—a college fraternity beer fest—ended before it began. Carless, Jim had asked his father to drive them to Jersey City. The party was on Bartholde Street not far from Journal Square. The directions were imperfect and the dark streets added more detours to their travels. Jim' father, Benny, was not an educated man. A longshoreman by trade, he was usually two sheets to the wind, especially on Saturday nights. After driving in circles for an hour, he stopped a passerby on the street to ask for directions. Even when sober, his Irish brogue made him difficult to understand, but with an excess of beer weighing down his tongue, he sounded incoherent.

"Hey... Hey... buddy. D'ya know where Bartho Dum Dum Street is?"

The emphasis placed on "Dum Dum" was all the incentive Jim needed to encourage his father to keep talking.

"Batho Dum Dum... Yeah, that's the street, dad." Jim swallowed hard to keep from laughing out loud.

Seated in the rear of the car, he continue to prod his father to say the street name again and again. Eventually, the passerby walked away contemplating the safety of the road with another drunken fool behind the wheel.

"Such a cruel sense of humor," Palma thought. The warning bells were sounding in her head but, once again, she silenced them.

Jim's parents never owned a new car. Instead, they bought one clunker after another from the local used car dealer. Palma was sure the guy was a shyster and Benny was his number one pigeon. Unfortunately, since Jim had no money and Palma was already inundated with bills, that shyster offered them the only affordable means of transportation. A chocolate brown Chevy impala was their chariot of choice. One week of ownership and the air conditioning died with a spit and a sputter.

Forced to ride with the windows open, the pummeling of the wind tore lose the interior roof lining. Duct tape held it in place for a few months. Eventually, engine trouble and the need for a new transmission relegated the car to the junkyard but not before another strong gust of wind ripped the lining completely free while they were doing 75 mph on the highway. The material completely encased their heads and shoulders, blocking all view of the road and nearly causing them to crash into a retaining wall. Only a second stronger gust of wind, which sent the lining flying out the passenger window, saved their lives. Palma and Jim were back to walking and taking the bus.

Once Palma and Jim were married, privacy became non-existent. She was forbidden to lock the bathroom door whether showering, using the toilet or applying makeup. Her one act of defiance resulted in a broken lock and splintered frame caused by Jim forcibly kicking the door open. For weeks afterward, her arms, bruised a deep purple, bore the imprint of Jim's fingers.

"I told you not to lock the door. You better start listening to me," Jim threatened while menacingly shaking her. He literally lifted her off the toilet, which she had not finished using.

Jim began to control every second of Palma's life. She was not permitted on a checkout line with a male cashier. Neither was she allowed to pass within a few feet of another man on the sidewalk. The situation was made worse by Jim's refusal to do any of the shopping by himself. He was too impatient to wait in line if more than one person was ahead of him. Complicated problems he could solve—defusing the atom bomb would have been child's play—but everyday inconveniences were intolerable to him.

Palma was rarely allowed to see her family and never without Jim being present. Isolation became a strong deterrent to rebellion. She was expected to work, clean, shop and pay the bills. Jim drank, partied with his friends and forged her name to credit card applications. Of course, Palma was totally unaware of the debt he was incurring until the bills flooded their mailbox—all in her name. So large was the amount they owed that there were weeks when a quart of milk was a luxury.

CHAPTER SEVENTEEN

Vain by nature, Jim grew more and more obsessed with his appearance—a small pimple becoming the cause for hysteria. He showered constantly and obsessively combed and re-combed his hair. Palma was expected to iron all his clothes... even his underwear. Jim preened in front of the mirror for hours before going out alone.

By contrast, he was a slob at home. After blowing his nose in the sleeve or hem of his undershirt, he would toss it on the floor, wadded up in a ball. Palma found his jockey shorts and socks under the sofa or the bed when the vacuum sucked them from their hiding places. Shoes remained wherever they landed when Jim kicked them off—one in the living room, one in the hallway or the kitchen.

Beginning on their wedding night, Jim became fixated on anal sex and seemed to find added pleasure in brutally forcing himself upon Palma. The first time was in the honeymoon suite shortly after leaving their reception. Grabbing Palma in an embrace that she thought was foreplay, Jim spun her around and threw her face down on the bed, pinning her arms over her head. Twisting and turning, she fought to get free until the pressure of Jim's knees on her thighs thwarted her efforts.

"You're hurting me. Stop!"

Jim's only response was to shove himself inside her, tearing the delicate skin. The weight of his body was suffocating. The more Palma struggled, the harder he pushed. When he was through, he rolled off her and went into the bathroom. He did not speak to Palma who, in pain and afraid to move, cried into a pillow. Returning to the bedroom, Jim turned on the television, clicking through station after station, to drown out her sobs.

Needing to clean herself and treat her injuries, Palma stood to remove her bloodied and stained peignoir. She was horrified at the condition of the beautiful no longer white chiffon gown that her sister had given her as a bridal shower gift. Seeing the pained expression on Palma's face and the timid way in which she moved, Jim laughed maliciously.

"I waited a long time for that. The only thing that could have made it more perfect would have been a big red bow on your ass."

Fearing a repeat performance, Palma remained quiet as she ministered to her bruised body. "I am losing my mind," she thought. "This can't be happening."

Jim continued to abuse Palma when she least expected it; even while his buddies waited in the living room to play a game of basketball. If Palma did not resist, he still raped her but with less pleasure. She learned not to resist. It was the only revenge available to her.

Palma soon learned the difference between love and possession. She wasn't a person to Jim; she was some thing—not someone—he owned. Jim needed Palma but he didn't want her. Neither did he want anyone else to have her. She belonged to him and him alone.

Whenever they went somewhere together, Palma was filled with dread. The more crowded the venue, the deeper her foreboding. Invisibility was a refuge denied to her. If a male, even a male with a woman at his side, smiled a "Good day," Jim immediately accused her of cheating on him. A nod from a passing stranger fueled an attack. He questioned her relentlessly about how she knew the man, what she had done with him and how often.

As watchful as Jim was, when Palma eventually did have an affair, he was clueless. By that time, his excessive drinking had distorted his mind to the point where he thought Palma was poisoning his food. He was rarely lucid and even more rarely at home anymore.

If ever an affair could be said to have a positive outcome, Palma's relationship with co-worker Bill Walker was it. Bill was a partner in the accounting firm where Palma worked. He was based in the New Orleans office and met Palma when he attended a companywide meeting at the Manhattan headquarters. That meeting led to a promotion and a permanent transfer to the Big Apple. Fate once again stepped in and changed the game plan for both of them. Bill was 14 years Palma's senior but the age difference meant nothing to her. He was young at heart and made her feel carefree for the first time in years.

The memory of their first meeting stayed strong long after the relationship ended, which was two years after they met. Whenever Palma heard, "Good morning, Sunshine," she smiled, remembering how Bill's eyes would sparkle every day when first seeing her. He renewed Palma's interest in having a better life and encouraged her to further her education. He made her laugh. They ate lunch together almost every day and whenever possible, they would sneak out of work early and enjoy an afternoon of carnal delight. Like grew into love but that love was not free of complications. Palma was still married to Jim and Bill had a wife and four children. He was honest from the beginning of their relationship that he had no intention of leaving them. He offered to find Palma an apartment and help her pay for it. He wanted to hire bodyguards to protect her from Jim. "I love you," he told her, "but I love my wife and kids, too."

Palma vividly remembered their first intimate encounter and always blushed at the memory. Her embarrassment had nothing to do with the lovemaking but rather the less than sexy clothing she was wearing. It was a typical February day and Mother Nature had the entire east coast in a grip that was frozen solid. Since Palma's commute to work took over an hour on public transportation, she had dressed for warmth not sex appeal. A stylish turtle neck sweater, classic wool slacks, gloves, scarf, and hideously patterned knee high argyle socks tucked into high heeled boots. Since she would not be removing her boots at the office, Palma never gave a thought to the socks until she found herself in a hotel room in mid-afternoon undressing for the first time in front of the man she loved and desired.

Of course, the socks were only an issue for her. Bill was too occupied with removing his own clothes to notice such a small detail, but to Palma those socks forever symbolized the inappropriateness of their relationship. On the outside, she and Bill looked like two professional business people working side by side without any hint of sexual tension. Underneath that carefully constructed image was a deeply erotic yearning... an electrical charge that crackled with powerful urges.

The relationship ended when Bill told Palma she would have to find a new job. He had no choice but to fire her. Their romance was becoming the talk of the office and was threatening his position in the hierarchy. Not even partners were allowed to break the "no fraternizing" rule.

At first, Palma was heartbroken, but years later she was very grateful that Bill had recognized that their age difference and disparate goals would have eventually driven them apart. Whereas Bill was a Beefeaters on the rocks with a twist kind of guy, Palma was a diet Coke kind of girl. Bill spent his weekends on the golf course while Palma spent them at the theater or in an art gallery. Bill was settled in his ways while Palma was still evolving. Their time together had given Palma a new confidence and a sense that she was valuable as a human being. She now had a sense of purpose. Even with Jim still a threat to her life, she was able to hold her head higher. For that she would always be grateful.

CHAPTER EIGHTEEN

On her first wedding anniversary, Palma was rushed to the hospital gasping for breath. She was suffering severe palpitations, nausea and blurred vision. The emergency room doctors diagnosed her with a brain tumor. She told them, "Bull shit!" Bolting from the bed over the doctors' protests, Palma dressed quickly and checked herself out of the hospital. Even without medical training, Palma recognized the signs of a nervous breakdown. That day marked the first of thousands of anxiety attacks that would plague her for the rest of her life.

Jim's physical attacks became more violent and less predictable. Palma was afraid to close her eyes. His attempt to suffocate her with a dry cleaning bag while she slept was a clear warning of escalating danger. Palma was constantly amazed at the strength she found to fight Jim off, clawing and kicking until he let her go. One night, the kitchen counter held an unlikely means of self defense—a large can of cat food. Running to escape Jim's grasp, she grabbed the can and threw it with all her might, not stopping to see if she had hit him. She knew by his curses that her aim was true.

"You bitch. You fucking bitch. I'll kill you."

Barefoot, Palma yanked her pocketbook and car keys off the hook by the front door and fled the apartment. Twenty minutes later, shivering with fright, she pounded on Aunt Edna's door. Never had her aunt's face been such a welcomed sight. Her loving embrace, a hot cup of tea and a warm bed helped to calm Palma's nerves.

In the morning, despite her aunt's pleas not to go back, Palma went home. Jim begged forgiveness and swore to stop drinking.

Palma needed to believe him. Where else did she have to go? Adrianna didn't want her and she had no money to start a new life on her own.

Three nights later, as Jim forced her face down onto the mattress and raped her again, Palma took command of her life. In the morning, she claimed to be too sick to go to work. As soon as Jim left for his job, she packed her clothes and personal items, including the bills, and left without looking back. For a few weeks, she moved between family members, always changing location in the hope that Jim would not find her. Then, her worst nightmare became a reality. Joe died and Palma moved back home with her mother.

Joe worried constantly about Palma's safety. He never went to sleep without first speaking to her on the phone. Every morning, fearing that she had not survived the night, he called her. While Palma appreciated his concern, she knew he was as unable to protect her from Jim just as he had been to protect her from Adrianna. Joe also knew that and awareness of his failure weighed heavily on his heart.

Traveling to work in Long Island on a New York City subway train, Joe had a heart attack and died. Palma, who also worked in Manhattan, had only just arrived in her office — had not even removed her coat — when Adrianna called with the news. She insisted that Palma go to the hospital where Joe had been taken... not that she would have needed to make that demand. Palma pushed the down elevator button, her head filled with troubling thoughts.

"Did I kill him? Would he still be alive if not for Jim and me?"

Her eyes moved across the patterned carpet covering the wide expanse of office space, stopping at the conference room beyond. She focused on the large plate glass windows, slightly frosted from the cold gusts of January wind that buffeted them. Dust particles danced, like tiny ballerinas, in the few remaining rays of sunlight. She watched them as though in a trance. The high shine on the mahogany table could be easily seen even from a distance. Palma envisioned the original watercolor landscapes hanging on the walls... images of warmth and beauty in an otherwise formulaic professional décor.

Sometimes during meetings, when discussions of profit and loss statements became tedious, Palma mentally wandered into those paintings to relieve the boredom. She returned to the meeting only at the insistent kicking of her ankles by one of her co-workers. Palma bore enough black and blue marks to attest to the regularity of those escapes from reality.

Like an unwelcomed visitor, the rhythmic clacking of finger-nails on a keyboard and the insistent ringing of a phone tumbled Palmed back to the present. Answering the phone had recently become a game of chance—good news or bad news... which would it be. Instead of money, Palma often thought, you wager your life by merely saying, "Hello." Today, bad news won.
Palma desperately wished she had not answered her phone. The hysteria in her mother's voice and her unrelenting sobs only added to Palma's misery.

Today, rather than joining her colleagues for happy hour, a weekly re-birthing ritual resulting from her breakup with Jim, Palma was heading for New York Hospital to identify her father's body. "... a sudden heart attack," her mother wailed, but Palma knew better.

"You finally did it, Dad," she whispered. "You finally wished yourself to death." Joe's mantra, "Maybe I won't be here tomorrow," had finally come true.

Palma did not love her father less for choosing the easy way out. He was her daddy. She had needed to know he would always be there for her and now he was gone. Just as with Nonna, she never had a chance to say, "I love you" one last time.

Bowing her head, Palma swallowed hard to hold back the tears that flooded her eyes and dampened her cheeks. Taking a tissue from her pocket, she wiped her nose. Then, with reluctance, she lifted her head and straightened her shoulders. Noticing the elevator light still lit, she silently prayed, "Don't come. Don't Come," and then, "Hurry up. Hurry up!" As if in answer, the grinding gears signaled the car's arrival. Palma looked once more toward the windows. Gone was the sun and with it the tiny specs of dust suspended in the air.

"I can no longer see the dust fairies but I know they are still there," she assured herself. "Just like I know that daddy and Nonna will always be with me."

With that comforting thought, Palma stepped into the waiting elevator. The descent to the lobby was quick; amazingly a taxi was waiting at the curb. Once inside the cab, she steeled herself against the horror to come. Turning his head ever so slightly, the driver nodded, watching Palma in the rear view mirror.

"New York Hospital on 34th. Please hurry. My father is dying."

Expressionless, the driver pulled away from the curb and signaled for a right turn. Palma huddled in the seat, pulling her coat tight around her body as though the fabric could shield her from pain. Although she felt Joe and Nonna nearby, at this moment she was all alone in the cold, dark cellar of her mind.

The ride to the hospital seemed endless—Manhattan traffic was bumper to bumper in every direction. A few remaining Christmas decorations still adorned the surrounding high rise office buildings, their bright colors and twinkling lights projecting a stark contrast to Palma's somber mood. The dust in the conference room had triggered early memories of her mother's obsessive need to Clean! Clean! Clean! as though cleanliness could wipe away the terrors that must have haunted her.

"Poor, mother." Palma thoughts were momentarily compassionate. "She has always defined herself how tight she could make the bed corners and how perfectly she could tie a bow as if doing things well made her a better person. But, no matter how hard she scrubs, she will never rub the blackness from her soul. God knows she has tried."

Arriving at the hospital, Palma was asked to wait for the emergency room doctor on call. She sat in the lounge, unable to stop her knees from shaking, and watched as a middle aged man with salt and pepper hair and a stiffness in his step approached her. A shiver ran up her spine when she saw the name tag on his lapel... Dr. Smiles. Fleetingly, the idea that Joe might not be dead crossed her mind. Just as quickly, her hopes were crushed by the tone of the doctor's voice as he extended his hand and offered, "I am very sorry for your loss."

Clenching her jaw to remain strong, Palma listened to a brief description of the circumstances surrounding her father's death. Witnesses stated that Joe had walked with them from the bus terminal to the subway token booth. He was in good spirits... had even told a few jokes. At the booth, Joe stopped to buy a week's worth of tokens. Then, with a farewell wave to those who were not traveling in the same direction, he slipped through the turnstile, got on his train, sat down and died. It was that quick. Despite efforts to revive him, the heart attack was instantly fatal.

Palma was led to the private room where her father's body waited. Walking along the corridor, she constantly pivoted her head, looking into the rooms on either side. A man sitting up in a bed near the door so resembled Joe that Palma again hoped. Pressure from Dr. Smiles' hand on the small of her back steered her further down the hallway.

Palma had grown strong from her conflicts with Jim, but the thought of seeing her father in permanent repose filled her with dread.

"I can't do this. I can't do this."

The words echoed silently in her head. Dr. Smiles lowered the draping covering Joe's body and stood back. Palma took a deep breath to steady her nerves. Joe's blue eyes were closed although there was no aura of sleep. His skin was the same color as his grey hair. His hands were cold to the touch. He wasn't smiling as he always did when she visited him. Palma sensed the finality of his leaving. With a tender kiss on his forehead and a gentle caress of his cheek, she said goodbye. She cried all the way home; the stares of strangers not stemming the flow of her tears.

CHAPTER NINETEEN

Joe's wake and funeral were a stand-alone horror story which began when Palma and Adrianna went to the funeral home to pick out a casket. The somber funeral parlor director, dressed in the requisite black, led them around a showroom that was more Thomasville than Hillenbrand—the company which manufactures and sells more than 800,000 of the 1.8 million caskets sold in the United States each year.

There were bouquets of flowers on exquisitely detailed end tables strategically placed to fool the customer into thinking they were shopping for a sofa rather than a bed for the dead. Tiffany lamps and overhead chandeliers provided a warm glow in an attempt to soften the cold reality that life meant eventual death. The funeral director was well-versed in the "special" features of each casket. First, he explained the different styles: pressed plywood covered with cloth, plywood covered in hardwood, high density wooden fiberboard painted with a wood veneer, and solid mahogany, walnut, cherry, maple, oak, poplar or pine.

Palma and Adrianna were also given the option of a steel coffin offered in 16, 18 or 20 gauge or, at the very high end of the price range, solid copper or solid bronze. The density of the mattress and pillow were also discussed along with differences in the linings—satin, velvet or polyester. Exterior features such as handles and ornamentation were the final choices that needed to be made. The funeral director pushed the high priced selections with the confident air of a used car salesman. "So what will it be for your loved one... a Pinto or a Cadillac?"

Palma found the entire discussion ludicrous. Her father had been a simple man more inclined to choose a cardboard box had he been given the choice. Worrying about whether or not he would rest more comfortably on a puncture resistant versus leak proof mattress was as ridiculous as it was distasteful. She encouraged her mother to choose mid-priced everything and headed for the door.

The wake was a fiasco—a nightmare situation made worse by Jim's presence. Under the guidance of a family friend, Palma had hired an attorney and filed for divorce. As she wanted only her freedom, she had agreed to pay off all the bills and take nothing from the apartment but her personal belongings. Jim would get all the furniture, appliances and wedding gifts. Palma was happy to be rid of them and the memories they held. Freedom was worth any price.

Although the divorce papers had been served, Jim was in denial, refusing to believe that Palma had the courage to see proceedings through to the end. He insisted on being present at the wake all three nights as a sign of his support and Adrianna, wanting to avoid further stress, agreed to ignore him. On the last evening, Jim arrived accompanied by his parents and an aunt and uncle. Palma was shocked to see them. Months had passed since they were last together. Devout Catholics, the family was adamant that Palma was committing a sin which would relegate her to the fires of hell... which was what they felt she deserved and where she felt she was already residing.

After extending his sympathies to Palma and Adrianna, Jim's uncle asked to speak to Palma alone. Ever the family attorney, a simple conversation with Uncle Johnny always felt like a cross-examination. Seated in the back of the room, he held Palma's hand while expressing his joy that a reconciliation was soon to be announced. "So, I hear that you and Jim are working through your problems. That's wonderful. Can we expect a baby in the near future?"

Palma's shocked expression was answer enough. Rocketing out of her chair, she advised Uncle Johnny that the divorce would be finalized as planned. Then, she stormed back to her mother's side at the front of the room. She refused to make eye contact with Jim. The clanging of the chairs announced the family's hasty departure.

Minutes later, Palma was forcibly grabbed by the back of her neck and dragged toward her father's coffin. Jim, enraged that his parents now knew the truth, threatened, "… to make the funeral a father/daughter affair."

"I will kill you before I let you shame me this way. Let's see how you like sharing that coffin with your father."

Only the quick reflexes of the funeral director, who was talking with Adrianna, and the actions of several male relatives prevented matters from escalating. Jim was tackled and carried out to the street, all the while screaming that he would punish Palma for humiliating him. Holding onto the side of the casket, Palma slid to the floor. She pulled her trembling legs to her chest. With her head bowed, much as it had been on her wedding day, she moaned, "Daddy, I need you so much."

In the confusion, Adrianna fainted and needed to be revived. She was being comforted by the priest who had arrived to say the evening prayers. Seeing that Palma was also in distress, Father Mark reached out to her. "Palma, are you all right?"

The question forced Palma to look up. Rage overcame her when she saw the priest holding her mother's hand. "Useless priest. Useless prayers," she spit out the words. Her face was distorted in anger as she struggled to her feet. Immediately, she was surrounded by caring friends, who offered their support and sympathy.

The funeral director locked the front doors and quickly es corted the remaining guests out the back of the building. Taking her mother home and getting her into bed kept Palma occupied for the next few hours. Exhausted, shaking and unable to sleep, she sat in a chair by her bedroom window and stared at the lone streetlight visible through the curtains. The alarm on her bedside table roused her at 6:00 am

At the funeral mass, security in the form of nephews and

cousins manned the doors of the church to prevent Jim from entering. Although he could be seen watching from a distance, he never approached Palma. At the cemetery, he stood where Palma could see him each time she raised her head to look at the gathered crowd. The look in his eyes was anything but sympathetic.

On the ride back from the cemetery, Palma reflected on how her life had been in constant turmoil—first because of her mother's cruelty, then Jim's erratic behavior and, now, her father's death. She marveled at her ability to rise each morning and go on with her life. Unfortunately, the moments when she was able to put all thought of Jim and her mother aside and enjoy just being young were rare.

CHAPTER TWENTY

The sound of the disc jockey dropping a new record onto the turntable brought Palma back to reality. She stayed in the present just long enough to stir Nonna's sauce to keep it from burning. The lyrics to Donna Sommers' pop hit *Bad Girls* called to her from the living room. The words sounded motivational... almost inspirational... and she could not keep her hips from swiveling along with the beat. Wine glass once again in hand, Palma returned to memories of the night before.

***

Kelso's Shanty Bar and Restaurant was vibrating as the DJ spun another beat heavy song and encouraged patrons to "Get up and dance." When Palma made her hasty departure from Jim, she promised herself that she would recapture the youth she had lost while engaged and married to him. She kept that promise every Friday night at the popular watering hole a few blocks from the office where she and her friends went to celebrate the end of another week. Most Fridays, Palma was excited to join the almost tribal-like communing that pulsated on the small dance floor.

Standing in the middle of the living room, Palma smiled remembering the excess of beer that had made the group livelier than usual. Paul and P. J. began dueling with the little plastic swords used to skewer the bite-sized hot dogs on the happy hour bar. Remnants of mustard splattered the table and their shoes, leaving a Jackson Pollack painting on their Mephisto loafers. Their behavior, so uncharacteristic for staid accountants working at one of the better known firms, made their comical actions even more hilarious.

As one song ended and another began, Palma was once again

transported back in time. There were nights when even the bohemian atmosphere of Kelso's could not protect her from the past. On those nights, the only sounds she heard were her own screams.

***

The banging of beer mugs on the table signaled another round of dinks being delivered by their favorite waitress, the divine Miss M... Maggie Mulroney. The sound startled Palma from her reverie.

"Hey, Palma," Maggie's Brooklyn accent ticked her ears. Her voice was a mix of elongated vowels and high pitched nasal intonations accented with a touch of Irish brogue. "You look like you've seen a ghost." Maggie's deep laugh was contagious. "Smile, girl. Get up and boogie, woogie, oogie with your friends."

"Long week, Maggs. Just need time to unwind."

A momentarily flustered Palma covered her discomfort by sipping her beer. Holding her glass aloft, she lifted her eyebrows and smiled, "Keep 'em coming. I'm feeling better already."

As Maggie walked away, her fingers formed an "OK " sign. Palma immediately returned to the past from whence she had abruptly returned.

***

"TGIF! TGIF!" Palma mouthed the phrase silently as she watched the digital minutes flip over on her desk clock. With tax season approaching, there was plenty of work to do and the morning hours flew. Federal and State Department of Revenue forms with deceptively simple titles cluttered her desk along with client financial statements and reports. Figures spun in her head with the speed of a Vegas roulette wheel. Arching her back to relieve the tension, Palma decided it was, "Time for a little break."

The weather was crisply inviting and a noon walk seemed a perfect way to refresh her mind and spirit. Moving along Sixth Avenue with the lunch crowd, Palma grew excited anticipating the "5:30 heft." That was what she and her friends called the first drink on a Friday night.

Louisiana born Bill, the senior accountant and Palma's lover, played master of ceremonies at the weekly festivities. A true Southern gentleman, genteel and soft spoken, Bill's speech was punctuated with colorful colloquialisms. A favorite was his reference to easy women, whose numerous relationships he equated to having "… more dicks than quills on a porcupine."

The first time Bill offered this observation, Dora, the normally reticent receptionist, challenged his assessment. Stating with feigned seriousness that easy women appealed to her alter ego, she offered the opinion that such findings needed to be scientifically validated. Rivers of tears zigzagged down the cheeks of those listening to the conversation as she described the requirements for men in the survey.

Dora, who spent her off hours volunteering at Bronx Zoo, was an expert on the behavior of male porcupines. For a human to replicate the mating process it would be necessary for a man to smell everything in close proximity to the female, paying special attention to objects which had come in contact with her genitalia and places where she had urinated. The male must then walk about the room holding his own genitalia in his left hand while rubbing himself on objects that the female had also touched. The larger the object, the more attractive a surface it became.

Ribald comments followed Dora's straight faced delivery and raucous laughter continued until another round of drinks was brought to the table—beer for Palma, Paul, P. J. and Dora… Beefeaters on the rocks with a twist for Bill. Lifting his martini glass with reverence, Bill officially ushered in the evening. "To porcupines—they bring a whole new meaning to foreplay."

"To porcupines," everyone cheered, raising their glasses in salute to the sharp quilled rodents.

Unselfconsciously, Palma mimicked her colleagues, holding her beer mug aloft. She smiled in anticipation of the evening ahead.

Palma's daydreaming was brought to a halt by the jostling of office workers anxious to return to their duties. With a bounce in her step, she pivoted back toward the accounting firm. Mid turn she sensed rather than saw Jim just as his strong hand gripped her shoulder. Tensing, Palma stared straight ahead. She considered running but knew she would not get far. Instead, she pleaded, "Please, go away, Jim. Please. Please, go away."

Glued to her side, Jim kept pace with Palma, all the while bantering about the weather and plans for the coming weekend. He held tightly—too tightly—to her hand. Only the arrival of lobby security guards on their regular rounds made it possible for Palma to escape without conflict. The day was ruined. Shortly after three, the threatening phone calls began as she knew they would. If not for the kindness of her immediate supervisor, Palma would be collecting unemployment. Jim's calls always started the same way—with him telling Palma how sorry he was for hurting her and swearing that she was his angel.

"When we have children," he promised, "I will tell them you are a gift from God."

Palma had given up reminding him of their impending divorce. Jim refused to hear her. She had stopped hanging up on him, knowing that he would call right back. Instead, Palma laid the receiver on the desk and continued working. The longer she remained silent, the more infuriated Jim became. In one breath, he morphed from adoring suitor to demented stalker.

"You fucking bitch. I'll kill you before I let another man have you."

Realizing that his loss of control would hamper his efforts to win her back, Jim reverted to the kind-hearted spouse he pretended to be. "I'm sorry, baby. The thought of losing you scares the hell out of me. I didn't mean what I said."

Even with the receiver two feet from her ear, Palma could hear him clearly. Every word was being preserved by the tape recorder next to the phone. On the advice of her lawyer, Palma had informed Jim that she was taping his calls. He thought she was bluffing and Palma had not assured him otherwise. Meant initially for use in the divorce proceedings, the tapes, somehow, made Palma feel she had a modicum of control.

From lover to liar, the one-sided verbal battle continued until quitting time, draining Palma emotionally. She begged off the Friday festivities, preferring home and the security of locked doors to the possibility of a public confrontation. The presence of other men only fueled Jim's anger and would endanger her friends. Spending the evening with her mother was far more appealing than ending the evening on a slab at the morgue. That threat was becoming more and more real with each passing day.

While driving aimlessly along the two lane cliff road near her home a few weeks earlier, Palma unexpectedly glimpsed Jim in her rearview mirror. She had little time to react before he began hitting her rear bumper, each jolt causing Palma to swerve right and left. Bile rose in her throat as she tried to maneuver the car along the narrow stretch and away from oncoming traffic.

When the road opened up enough to allow another car to pass, Jim veered into the left land and pulled level with Palma's vehicle. Slowly, he edged closer, forcing Palma into the guard rail. Afraid to look anywhere but straight ahead, she gripped the steering wheel tightly. She could hear the metal barricade etching deep grooves into the side of her car and prayed it was strong enough to prevent her from cascading over the edge into the river far below.

The blaring of a horn startled Palma, forcing her to look once again into the rearview mirror. From farther down the hill, the driver of an Edison Power and Light truck had seen her predicament and raced to her rescue. Laying heavily on his horn, the driver made it clear that Jim was now the target of his aggression. Not wanting to answer for his actions, Jim sped past Palma and out of sight. With a thumbs up, the driver stayed close behind Palma until she emerged onto the busy highway above.

CHAPTER TWENTY ONE

"Palma! Palma!"

The sound of her name being called over and over again brought Palma back to the current time and place.

"Come on Palma," Paul pleaded. "Dancing is no fun without my regular partner. Fred Astaire is nothing without Ginger Rogers."

Normally, one smile from Paul and Palma practically levitated to the dance floor. They were the best of friends, joined by shared interests including dancing—their favorite activity for relieving stress. On this night, Paul's smile, although endearing, only succeeded in getting a promise of "Later." Watching him weave his way back to the dance floor, Palma again retreated into her thoughts. She recalled a recent night that Jim had ruined with his threats, forcing Palma to forever be leery about traveling alone.

***

The subway entrance was one long block from the office. Hurried steps and a few backward glances brought Palma to her destination only slightly out of breath. The local train could be heard rumbling through the tunnel as it approached the station. With practiced familiarity, Palma stood far enough away from the edge of the platform to, hopefully, guarantee her safety and close enough to allow access to a car once the doors opened. Her senses on high alert, she watched and listened, prepared to run if the need arose. Her lawyer's warning bounced off the corners of her mind.

"Don't go anywhere alone, Palma. It's not safe."

Looking at the ever growing crowd, Palma rationalized, "Safety in numbers." In the oppressive heat of the station, the mingled scents of perfume, aftershave and perspiration were nauseating. She covered her nose with her hand to block the odors. The worn leather smell of her gloves was comforting. Above the clatter of the incoming train, Palma clearly heard the tapping of high heels on the metal subway stairs. Bodies pressed more closely against her and the platform became more crowded as nearby offices emptied for the day. All around her, commuters sniffled and sneezed with staccato precision—like tubas in a high school marching band. On tiptoe, Palma scanned the crowd for a glimpse of Jim. It was not unusual for him to follow her home from work.

Taller than most men, Jim stood out in a crowd. Palma knew she should have waited for her co-workers. Like her, they were commuters living in New Jersey who traveled hours through the darkening night to get home… first the subway train to Port Authority, then a bus to Bergen County.

"Safety in numbers," Palma reminded herself.

On this evening, when a birthday party had been planned for Patti, it would have been unfair to expect anyone to escort her home. Palma had been invited; Patti was a good friend; but she did not want to risk Jim suddenly appearing and ruining what was sure to be a fun night for everyone. She resented his control over her life and knew that if she had gone to the party, she would now be surrounded by a battalion of supporters rather than battling shadows like a lone infantryman.

Jim's threats had had the desired effect. Without her body guards, Palma was scared to death. Her office pals had become very protective since Jim began lurking in the lobby. He wasn't there every day but often enough to keep Palma on edge, which they did. A smile creased the corners of her mouth as she thought of Bill, P. J., Paul, Dora and Patti. The guys, dressed in nearly identical business uniforms—glen plaid suits, wing tip shoes and khaki overcoats—were her personal army. Patti and Dora claimed they could do more damage with a high heeled pump than the guys could do with a pump rifle.

Despite the physical and emotional pain Jim had caused, Palma still could not accept the psychiatrist's diagnosis. An exceptionally handsome man, well spoken, educated, with a high IQ, Jim should have been the perfect mate. But, according to Dr. Brant, "Jim is a very sick, very angry man, unable to function in the real world. You are the target for all his frustrations."

Once Palma had gotten the diagnosis of schizophrenia, she began to do some research. It was important for her to understand just what the condition meant and how it had come to be. Dr. Brant had equated the symptoms to a normal brain on overdrive. He said that at least one percent of the population would suffer from the mental disorder at some point in their lives. A significant number of people heard voices or suffered from hallucinations; others were riddled with strange ideas and believed that people could read their minds or were plotting to hurt them.

Palma spent many after work hours at the library. Her reading gave her some insights but not enough to explain why Jim had suddenly gone from angel to devil. One study suggested that personalities showed marked changes between adolescence and early adulthood when the brain was making "adjustments" to how it functioned. Dr. Brant equated it to a carpenter who is trying to level a piece of wood. He removes a little from the top and a little from the bottom. It's still not perfect so he removes a little more and a little more and a little more. Eventually, the top and bottom may be perfectly matched but too much wood has been planed away to make it useful. Since Jim had been normal when Palma first met him in high school and did not show any inclination to violence until a few years after graduation, that hypothesis seemed reasonable.

Try as she might, Palma could never leave the past behind. Standing on the subway platform, the weight of the memories caused her shoulders to tremble as a chill slithered down her spine. It had been so difficult to discuss the painful and embarrassing attacks Jim rained upon her with Dr. Brant, but she knew if she didn't get professional help… if she could not understand why Jim had changed… that she would be doomed to the dungeon of despair for the rest of her life.

Palma heard Dr. Brant's words so clearly he could have been standing next to her. "Your husband exhibits all the classic signs of paranoid schizophrenia. It is my opinion that he has latent homosexual tendencies as well. These books…" Dr. Brant swept his arm toward the shelves lining the walls of his office, "… are filled with case histories exactly like yours."

Palma had replayed that conversation over and over again in her head. When she did not respond to Dr. Brant's words, he had come around the desk to sit beside her. With the intensity of a Supreme Court judge rendering a decision, he said, "Jim could commit suicide if life's pressures become too great. Yet, he is equally capable of killing you as the imagined cause of those pressures. Please, don't become a statistic." Again indicating the bookshelves, he advised, "Get protection and get a divorce. Now!"

Palma was still reeling from those words. Mental instability she could accept. Jim's childhood, like Palma's, had not been easy, but the idea that he was a homosexual seemed unfathomable. Jim hated homosexuals. Barely a day passed without his demeaning comments and solemn protestations that gays would burn in hell. More than once she wondered if she had been missing the message all along.

Initially refusing to believe the psychiatrist, Palma made a last resort appointment to speak with the priest who had officiated at their wedding. Father Patrick had known Jim since his days as an altar boy at Our Lady of Grace Church. Palma, clinging to the sanctity of the sacraments, wanted desperately to save her marriage. The priest listened to her story with obvious disbelief. He dismissed her, verbally pushing her out the door.

"I've known Jim all his life. This is your fault. Go home and be a better wife."

Emotionally devastated by Father Patrick's rejection, Palma felt abandoned. In a desperate last ditch effort to save her marriage, she decided to invite Jim to meet her at their favorite Mexican restaurant. Her intention was to... Palma didn't really know what she intended to do. She just wanted an explanation.

The dinner was a disaster. With the expertise of a master actor, Palma had casually broached the subject of Jim's sexuality. She cautiously explained Dr. Brant's diagnosis and silently willed Jim to deny that he was gay... and he did. Red faced, fists clenched, half out of his chair, his denial was so vehement that it blared confirmation. As he leaned across the table snarling hot breathed protests into Palma's face, she had recoiled in fear. Dr. Brant's warning no longer seemed implausible. The risk of exposure was too great for Jim's Irish Catholic sensibilities. Better a murderer than a homosexual was the clear message he was sending.

***

Pressed by the crowd, Palma jolted back from the edge of darkness. As the subway train pulled to a screeching stop, she ruminated, "Will I live to add another day to my 23 years? It seems a dark cloud has been hanging over my head ever since the doctor swatted my backside in the delivery room."

That smack had been a portent of the harsh life ahead.

***

116

CHAPTER TWENTY TWO

"Later is now, Palma. Come on. Dance with me. You'll forget that bastard for awhile."

Palma was startled by the nearness of lips to her ear. She stiffened until she realized it was Paul, whose persistence was well known in the office. He pulled Palma's chair away from the table and offered her his hand. Palma stood and followed him to the center of the dance room.

Moving comfortably against Paul, the beat filled Palma's body. Hips swaying with the music, she felt as if she was being transported to a place far away... a place free from worry and care. Maybe it was the music. Maybe it was the beer. Whatever was causing the euphoria that was spreading through her limbs, she was grateful for the respite, knowing that she would not be able to avoid the memories and the worry on the long ride home.

Despite the freedom of movement Palma felt while in Paul's arms, her mind and her heart remained heavy. She longed to just embrace the moment, but she knew that, if she did not keep one eye on the door, the moment could end in a rush of fists, foul language and filthy accusations. She'd been here too many times before—times when she had let down her guard and allowed herself to be happy only to have Jim come through the front door like Satan on a mission. She hoped that her ruse... she had hinted to Jim that she would be taking a night course at the local college... would keep this evening from turning into a segment on the 11 o'clock news.

Wanting nothing more than to be young, carefree, and yes, even careless for just a few hours, Palma threw herself into the frenetic beat of the merengue that blared from the sound system. She and Paul were known to clear the dance floor with their perfectly executed moves. The merengue was Palma's favorite dance. There was, she believed, something primitive and, yet, regal in the way the upper body was held stiffly posed while the hips and legs carried the dancers around the floor with abandon.

Palma and Paul had done this dance together so often that they anticipated each other's moves. They were one person in body and mind. Legs and hips in constant motion, they circled each other—chest to chest/back to back—in perfect rhythm. For couples involved in an intimate relationship, the movements took on a decidedly sexual overtone. Palma avoided that suggestion by keeping a bit of distance between her body and Paul's body. Still, there was something about the way they looked at each other… not lustfully but hungrily… not predator and prey. The bar patrons were also caught up in that stare. They could not turn away. Many swayed with the music mimicking the dancers they were watching. Then, the music ended and Palma and Paul fell away from each other laughing with delight and effectively breaking the spell they had cast on the room.

It was almost midnight when the DJ announced "… last song." The friends gathered their belongings and headed out the door. Tired but happy yawns creased their faces as they discussed their travel options. Only Dora lived on the New York side of the Hudson River. Giving each of the others a quick hug of farewell, she hurried toward the subway station and home. Palma, Bill, T.J., Paul and Patti decided to splurge on a cab; the night being too cold for walking. Giggling, all but Bill squeezed into the back seat. Being the senior member of the group, he was given the honor of sitting in front with the driver.

As was often the case after a long, hard week of work, the effects of the last few frivolous hours took hold. A comfortable silence settled over the friends. Staring out the cab windows, they watched the street numbers whiz by as the taxi sped along Sixth Avenue. Arriving at Port Authority Bus Terminal, they quickly divvied up the fare, passing the money to Bill. Once on the sidewalk, they linked arms, bowed their heads against the wind and rushed inside the terminal.

Arriving at Platform 54, the sight of passengers already boarding the bus forced the friends to walk faster. With Bill ever in the lead, they moved toward the rear of the coach, securing five seats adjoining each other. Bill and Palma sat together with Palma taking the aisle seat since she got off first. Patti and Paul sat in front of them. T.J. sat alone, across the aisle, turning in his seat so he could talk to the others.

"You seemed to have fun tonight, Palma. It did my heart good to hear you laugh." Bill reached for Palma's hand and held it gently in his own; their affection for each other hidden by the high seat backs. "I wish we didn't need to pretend that our relationship was strictly collegial. I want to be the man pressing his hips against yours on the dance floor."

"I know it looks as if I'm totally into Paul while we're dancing, but it's you I'm thinking about."

"As much as you might think about me, you also can't stop thinking about Jim."

"That would be a foolish mistake. I doubt he ever stops thinking about me… about how he can make my life even more miserable than he has up to now."

"And that's what occupied your thoughts on the ride over here, isn't it? You were very quiet in the cab. I knew you were dreading the bus ride home."

"Too many thoughts. Too many fears. Too many hours trying to prevent the inevitable."

"If, by inevitable, you mean Jim hurting you… No. There has to be a way to stop him. You are an amazing woman. The strength you have shown over the past year is admirable. I don't know that I would be as brave as you."

"It isn't bravery, Bill. It's survival skills. I've been honing them since the day I was born." Palma lowered her voice so the others would not hear. "Having you in my life has given me strength I didn't know I had."

"Has your life been that difficult? You never talk about your family... except for your grandmother... not even when the rest of us are complaining about our own."

"Difficult, yes, but others have known worse. The details would bore you."

"I wish I had known your grandmother. When you speak of her... well, it's obvious she was and still is the center of your universe. You and your Nonna... two saints in a troubled world."

Palma offered an appreciative laugh. She rested her head back against the seat and turned to look out the window, shutting off all further conversation. Her hand was still nestled gently inside Bill's closed fingers.

As the bus lurched and pulled away from the curb, Patti, Paul and T.J. settled back in their seats. The interior coach lights dimmed, but rather than casting Palma into the dark realm of depression as she had expected, the semi-darkness sparked a sudden awareness. Hanging from the platform walls, poster-sized billboards advertising stores and restaurants inside or near the Port Authority Bus Terminal were lit by overhead neon lights. One very colorful advertisement caught Palma's attention. It was for a popular Italian restaurant and depicted a huge plate of pasta with two globe-sized meatballs on top. Scattered about the white cloth-covered table on which the pasta bowl sat were open spice bottles labeled basil and oregano, cloves of garlic and pine cones split in half so as to reveal their hidden treasure... pignoli nuts. The caption read "Mangia!"

Suddenly, the solution to all her problems with Jim became crystal clear. Palma had had the way out of her dilemma all along and never realized it until this moment.

CHAPTER TWENTY THREE

Like an oft seen rerun of a favorite television show, Palma played out in her mind the evening ahead. She knew every action, every word of dialogue, every prop. Hearing the door bell ring, she put down her wine and hurried to grant her guest entry.

Without much in the way of greeting, Jim brushed past Palma and took up a predatory position, slouching in the kitchen doorway to watch her cook. His body held the familiar hawk-like stance comfortably. His stare, which followed Palma with intense scrutiny, confirmed that paranoia controlled his thinking. Palma knew that no matter how many times she seasoned and tasted the food, Jim would not be convinced that it was harmless.

After wiping away whatever bits of evidence remained on the cutting board and the blobs of sauce that had bubbled over onto stove top, Palma completed the preparations for dinner. She turned the heat up under Nonna's big old pasta pot, added salt and a tablespoon of olive oil and put the lid in place. She poured wine into each of the glasses on the dining table. Then, she quickly prepared the salad dressing and motioned for Jim, who was still leaning against the kitchen door jamb like a juvenile delinquent, to take his seat.

"Shall we toast?" Palma picked up her glass. Jim did not answer nor did he make a move to join her at the table. Since the appetizer had already been served, Palma picked up her fork and began to eat in silence. Jim watched and waited. After she had taken a few mouthfuls, he sat down and picked up his own fork. He ate but remained ever cautious… watching to make sure that Palma ate every morsel.

Next came the salad course. Palma filled both of their plates with the fresh mix of greens, fruits and nuts. She shook the bottle holding the dressing and poured some on her salad before adding a few of the blue cheese crumbles. All the while, she could feel Jim's eyes burning into her. Trying to remain calm, she looked at him for confirmation that he wished to be served.

"May I pour the dressing for you?"

"You eat first."

Palma did as instructed; then looked again at Jim for instructions.

"I can pour my own." Jim reached for the dressing bottle, shook it, studied the contents, then uncapped it and poured some onto his salad.

The meal continued. Conversation was forced but Palma did her best to keep the topics light and convivial. "So, Jim, how are you doing in your new job? Is it as challenging as you hoped it would be?"

"They're all idiots... never met such stupid people... but the job pays the bills."

"Well, it's always nice to take home a pay check and, if you want to look for a new job, it's good to be able to do so from a position of power."

"Uh huh."

"Jim, I was hoping we could talk about our situation. Perhaps, find a resolution that works for both of us."

"What needs to be resolved? Either you'll move back in with me or I'll move in here with you. End of story."

Palma felt a tightening in her chest. She fought to hold back her tears and keep the frustration out of her voice. The sound of the pot lid rattling gave Palma the excuse she needed to leave the table. The steam pressure building inside the scratched and dented silver cauldron was analogous with the hatred building inside of her. She smiled and excused herself, quickly turning her back to Jim so he would not see the anger in her eyes. At the stove, she lifted the pot lid and carefully added the spaghetti to the rolling rapids. With a wooden spoon in one hand and her wine glass in the other, she stirred the long thin spaghetti noodles and prayed, "Let there be salvation in the wheat, the nut and the grape."

"Just a few more minutes, Jim. I made Nonna's delicious meatballs. I even added ground pignoli nuts. I know how much you like them. Did you notice I put some in the salad as well?"

"Uh huh."

The familiar routine of switching plates began when Palma served the main course. Jim watched as she strained the pasta, added a portion to their plates, ladled sauce on top and placed them on the table. She replaced the vase of flowers with a separate bowl of meatballs.

"May I serve you, Jim"

"Sure."

Palma put two of the tasty orbs on Jim's plate and then did the same for herself. She sat down and began to eat. Jim did not pick up his fork until Palma had swallowed a few bites of meatball and a forkful of pasta. Then, he reached across the table, switched their plates and chowed down.

Palma refilled her wine glass and poured more for Jim, a small smile creasing the corners of her mouth. "I'm so glad you agreed to join me for dinner, Jim. We've been fighting for too long." Twirling another forkful of pasta against the bowl of her spoon, Palma offered a review of the meal she had so carefully prepared, "Ummmm. The sauce and meatballs are really good tonight. Nonna's extra special recipes. Doesn't everything taste wonderful?"

"Uh huh."

"If this were my last meal on earth, I'd die a happy woman. Would you like another serving?"

"Sure. I'll have a little more… and another meatball."

"My pleasure."

"My plate. Your plate. Any plate… it makes no difference to-night." Palma bit down on her tongue for fear of speaking the words out loud. Instead, she raised her glass in a toast. "Peace."

EPILOGUE

2015

When Diana Ciccone entered Claudia Allerd's office, the attorney was immediately struck by her new client's beauty. Yes, she was older, but there was no denying that the fictional Palma Domenica Rigo and the author were one and the same. Once the pleasantries of introduction were over, Ciccone wasted no time in revealing the reason for her visit.

"My ex-husband is trying to kill me."

"Have you actually received a death threat?" Allerd, the most high-powered female attorney in the country, held a copy of Ciccone's book, *Private Hell*, in her hands.

"If you're asking if he's actually said, 'I'm going to kill you,' the answer is no."

"Then what makes you so sure he wants you dead?"

"Trust me. I know."

"Your ex-husband... he's the man you wrote about in your book... the man you murdered by feeding him meatballs made with ground castor beans?"

"Yes. Ricin is a poison found in castor beans. When the beans are chewed and swallowed, the poison is released. After ingestion, the effects of ricin poisoning usually appear within 10 hours. They can range from fever, coughing, difficulty breathing and tightness in the chest to fluid in the lungs, respiratory failure and death. Death usually occurs within 36 to 72 hours of eating the beans."

"Feeding someone castor beans is a clever way to commit murder. You would be long gone before the symptoms were evident and even farther away by the time of death."

"Yes, but it's not like I actually did it. I only murdered him in the book... killed myself as well in case you missed that fact. Until recently, I hadn't seen Brad in over 42 years."

"Mrs. Ciccone... Diana... you'll have to be tolerant of my questions. They aren't meant to intimidate you or question your narrative of events. It's obvious you're scared, but if I am to help you, I need to know how and why you feel your life is being threatened. I also need to know why you are so sure a ghost from your past is responsible."

"I know it's Brad... Jim in the book. He's been watching me. Always from a distance."

"He's never approached you? Never spoken to you?"

"No, but everything that is happening to me has happened before. I feel as though I've entered a time warp where the past and present have been reversed."

"And, you believe, this is because of your book?"

"*Private Hell* has gotten a lot of press and Brad is, no doubt, furious that I used our relationship as the basis for my story. When I began writing the book, I did worry about his reaction should he ever read it."

"But you went ahead with the story anyway."

"Yes. I took the precaution of writing under an assumed name—Ms. Marjorie Markel—an homage to Agatha Christie's Miss Marple. Truthfully, I thought it far-fetched that anyone would make the connection between us but just to be sure, I checked obituaries and city records to see if his parents were still alive. They're not, and a younger sister has also passed away. That leaves another sister and a brother. The risk seemed small that they would read *Private Hell* and know that Ms. Markel was me."

"And, yet, he found out."

"To quote Lemony Snicket, "Assumptions are dangerous things to make, and like all dangerous things to make... if you make even the tiniest mistake, you can find yourself in terrible trouble.""

"And so you have."

"It seems that way."

"When you were doing your research, did you learn anything about Brad? Is he remarried? Does he have children?"

"I don't know. I read a ten-year old newspaper article on the internet about a woman doing charity work. She lived in New Jersey and was married to a Brad McDonald. There were no photos... no links."

"All right. For the sake of this discussion, let's say your ex has read your book and he's out for blood. Why?"

"Brad was always vindictive. It's possible he has never forgiven me for divorcing him. I'm sure it was a humiliating time even though his family blamed me. He either wants revenge or money... probably both."

"What you wrote... it's all factual?"

"Yes. Well, not the murder part. Obviously, I didn't kill anybody, but the abuses... all that I described and many that I didn't were painfully real."

"You obtained your divorce in 1973?"

"Yesterday."

"I don't understand."

"The ravages of domestic abuse never fade. Even though the abuse happened a lifetime ago, the emotional scars remain visible. Ask any survivor. You will hear my words repeated back to you verbatim. Women who survive domestic abuse get good at playing the part of confident female. Some days, the act doesn't take much effort. Time hones our performance skills. Routine tasks that are taken for granted by other people—going to the post office or grocery store—are major accomplishments for us. Leaving the house after dark... For me, that's still a work in progress. I rarely pump gasoline because gas stations are male heavy businesses. I always feel exposed and vulnerable while waiting for the tank to fill. Thankfully, my husband, Mitch, understands and handles that chore."

"So, you're telling me that four decades after divorcing Brad, you're still tormented by the memories of those years?"

"Yes."

"Then, why write the book and open old wounds?"

"That misconception... the belief that the memory of abuse fades once a woman breaks free... is the reason so many survivors never get the help they need. Our wounds are the kind that never heal. They're like a flesh eating virus. They fester and infect all aspects of our lives. I wish I had a penny for every night's sleep I've lost, every anxiety attack when the urge to throw myself out a window was so strong I was forced to grip a door jamb or the arms of a chair to keep myself steady, every dog bark that caused grey hairs to sprout on my head and every loud noise that caused my heart to jump into my throat. If I had those pennies, I'd be a very rich woman but I'd still as petrified as I am right now."

"You are also a very brave woman Writing *Private Hell* must have been emotional torture."

"It wasn't easy revisiting the past in such detail. I've often referenced my experiences when talking to survivors but, truthfully, for self-preservation purposes, I've learned how to compartmentalize. When I talk about those years, it's as though they happened to a different Diana Ciccone. Seeing the words in print made it all real again."

"Did you ever consider stopping?"

"Not just considered. I did stop. Many times. I always went back. I've never been willing to let the past define or defeat me, and I've always been too impatient to sit alone in a room and dwell on my troubles."

"That's an interesting perspective. '...too impatient to sit alone in a room.' What does that mean?"

"I'm a doer. When I know a wrong needs to be righted, I... I know that one person cannot repair all that is wrong in the world but, maybe, one person can hammer out one dent... smooth out one rough spot. I'm hoping this book will open, at least, one set of eyes."

"I'm curious. How long did it take to complete *Private Hell*?"

"Eight hundred and fifty two days. I marked every one of them off on a calendar and I swear to you, there wasn't one day when I didn't feel like I had gone 12 rounds with Mohammed Ali. It was a very rude awakening to learn that no matter how fast and how far I have run these last four decades, the past was still just one step behind me. I'll bet when Billy Rose penned *Me and My Shadow*, he never thought of it as an anthem for abused women."

"I don't understand."

"Like the wallpaper sticks to the wall
Like the seashore sticks to the sea
You'll never get rid of your shadow
You'll never get rid of me."

"I don't believe I've ever heard that version."

"It was a duet sung by Frank Sinatra and Sammy Davis, Jr. Appropriate, don't you agree? One of the things I love about being a writer is being able to manipulate the meaning of words. However, I could have done without this interpretation."

"So, 42 years after your divorce from Brad, you're still stuck with him."

"As I said earlier, because I've been so happy since I married Mitch, I sometimes think that my childhood and my first marriage were imagined. Writing the book forced the big, bad boogey man out from under the bed and made me accept that gone does not mean forgotten. *Private Hell* was a pinch so very painful that I could no longer pretend those abuses hadn't happened to me.

"I've read your book, but I do want to hear about your life from your lips. Leave out the literary narration. Just talk to me as if you were talking to an old friend."

"My childhood was not the stuff of fairy tales unless you are referring to Cinderella. The first 25 years of my life were hell on earth and, at the time, hell was located in Hudson County, New Jersey. It might still be there. My mother was abusive and the physical and emotional pain she caused was not conducive to raising a child with a lot of self confidence. At 17, I met a young man I mistook for my knight in shining armor, someone who would protect me from the evil queen. I married him at 21 and on our wedding night, the mask he wore fell away. I discovered, quite brutally I might add, that he was actually more frightening than the parent I was running away from. Eventually he was diagnosed as a paranoid schizophrenic with latent homosexual tendencies.

Let me be clear. I have no idea whether he was... is... actually a homosexual. That's the diagnosis a psychiatrist gave me when I went in search of answers to Brad's bizarre behavior.

I was also seeking an annulment from the Catholic Church and the first step was to have myself declared fit for marriage by a qualified therapist. The church had a lot of stupid rules in those day. Still does.

"I'm not familiar with the annulment process. Can you explain it to me?"

"The first step was to meet with my parish priest to get the paperwork started. He suggested I bring a check for $5,000. The money always seemed like a bribe to me. If you think the government moves slower than a sloth, try getting the Catholic Church to do something it is fundamentally opposed to regardless of the reason. Months and months passed before I was given a date to appear before a tribunal.

I have a pretty good idea of how people accused of a crime they didn't commit feel when on trial for their life. Threatened and embarrassed does not even begin to cover the range of emotions I experienced during the proceedings. For starters, as the applicant, I had to testify before a panel of three priests, who basically served as the jury. There was also a court stenographer -- another male -- who took notes. I type over 110 words a minute and his fingers flew across the keyboard putting my skills to shame.

The church was represented by another priest, the prosecutor, but I was not allowed any representation. My two witnesses... yes, I had to bring witnesses to back up my story because... well, the impression I got was that they felt all women are liars. Anyway, my witnesses were not allowed to accompany me into the hearing room. Alone and scared, I faced five stone faced men, who cared nothing about me or my plight. Forget water boarding. If you truly want to torture someone, humiliation is a very effective tool for breaking their spirit. Any confidence I felt was sucked out of me with the first question."

"What did they ask you?"

"They started with 'How often did you refuse to have sex

with your husband?' How ridiculous! What made them think I ever refused? I was still wondering whether and how to answer when I was gut punched with the next three.

'Have you ever given your husband a hand job?'

'Have you ever participated in anal sex?'

'Tell me, Mrs. McDonald, do you engage in oral sex?'

By this time, I was crying hysterically and could barely form words. I wanted to know why they were asking such personal questions. What was their relevance? And, by the way, I wasn't Mrs. McDonald anymore. My state divorce was final and I had taken back my maiden name, but they refused to use it."

Claudia Allerd was a captive audience, not because she had no means of escaping Diana's recitation but because she had no desire to leave. The lawyer realized that what Diana Ciccone was telling her would prove to be invaluable in years to come. Due to the recent revelations about pedophile priests, the Church was finding itself faced with many indefensible indictments. Allerd knew that crimes against women could not be far behind.

"Diana, do you want to take a break?"

"No. No. I might forget something."

"Take your time."

"The hearing became a circus. I could not understand how the questions they were asking had anything to do with me being able to form a marriage bond. The prosecutor priest said, 'Their relevance is for us to decide. Do you want an annulment or not?' It was a direct threat.

I don't mean to sound vulgar, but I swear the three priests on the dais were pleasuring themselves under the table. The only reason for asking those questions was to subjugate me. Do you know why I am so sure of their motives? When Brad sat before that same panel to refute my accusations, he wasn't asked one single question about our sex life. The psychiatrist I saw had written a report and in it, he voiced the possibility that Brad was gay, yet, no one asked him if he was.

In all the years that have passed since that incident, I haven't seen any progressive changes in the Catholic Church. Men who are isolated from the real world still dictate control over women's bodies. They still tell women to surrender themselves to their husbands. Men hold most positions of authority within a congregation. Women are relegated to doing menial labor. It's gender slavery.

When was the last time you saw a nun wearing a habit? When was the last time you saw a nun... period? Maintaining convents was an expense the church didn't want to absorb so many orders were pink slipped into oblivion. Did you know that, during the time nuns wore habits, they had to bind their breasts tightly to their chest so that any sign of sexuality was hidden? Many of them got breast cancer. Do you remember how they had to cover every inch of their bodies with the exception of their face, as though there was something shameful in being female?

Recently, I met a woman who had given 25 years to the Franciscan Order. When the hypocrisy of the Church's teachings became more than she could bear, she returned to civilian life. Twenty-five years with one company, so to speak, and what did she have to show for it? Two hundred dollars and a kick in the ass.

With that measly amount, she had to find a place to live, buy food and clothing, learn to drive, get a car and insurance, secure employment and begin the process of living not as some fictitious servant of God but as herself. She never lost faith, but she did think differently about the Church. I listened to her speak about how difficult it was to leave the second class citizen mentality behind and begin the process of believing that she was a capable and valuable individual. Somehow, she found the strength to pursue her dreams, and, more importantly, to realize she was entitled to those dreams.

Regina is a teacher now, teaching life skills to abused women, especially those with minority status. She also advocates for them to make sure they get all the benefits they are entitled to receive. You would like her. Regina's a big believer in the Equal Rights Amendment.... just like you. She has taken her own life lessons and turned them into a praise worthy curriculum. She's my hero."

"I'm sure she's a wonderful role model for the women she helps."

"Yes. She is." Diana stood and walked to the office window which looked out upon a roof top garden. Her shoulders shook as she tried to put the memory of the annulment back into its box. Claudia allowed her time to compose herself. When she was ready to continue their conversation, Diana returned to her seat.

"Earlier you said there was a possibility that Brad was a homosexual. Can you elaborate?"

"I mentioned the possibility of his homosexuality not as a condemnation but as an explanation for why he was such a troubled soul. Raised in a heavily Irish Catholic family, he may have felt forced to lie to himself and the world about his sexual identity. Society wasn't anywhere near as accepting in those days as it is now. There are so many stories... sad stories... that I could tell you about how emotionally tortured he was, but they are not meant for today's discussion. Suffice it to say that despite the physical and emotional pain he caused me... despite the fact that I am lucky to be alive... I do not blame him.

Although that part of my life happened a long time ago, I remember it all like it was yesterday and, thankfully so, because those memories have given me the insights I need to help abuse survivors. Do I wish my life had been different? Of course, I do! Given the chance, would I go back in time and change what happened? Absolutely... not! I would live every painful moment again because that experience made me who I am today... and today is all that matters.

I should interject here that for the past 42 years, I have been married to my real knight in shining armor. My husband, Mitchell, is a patient man. He allowed me to heal at my own pace and never asked more of me than I could give. He taught me to trust again."

"Diana... I have to say that, considering all you went through—your childhood and your time with Brad—I'm amazed you wanted to remarry."

"Me, too. I didn't at first. In fact, I would tell my friends that the only men I was interested in were those with one foot in the grave and the other on a banana peel. I also wanted them to have large life insurance policies and no beneficiaries but me."

"That's cold but understandable."

"My heart was pretty much an ice box."

"What changed?"

"After my father passed away, I went home to live with my mother. I didn't want to... I didn't relish being the new topic of conversation in the old neighborhood, but I really couldn't see a way out. She couldn't be left alone and who else was going to take care of her. Being Catholic, mom had memorial masses said every Sunday in our parish church, and she expected me to attend.

At the very first service, I looked around and saw, seated across the aisle, a boy—now a man—with whom I had gone to grammar school. He acknowledged me by raising one of his eye brows and when mass was over, he went out of his way to find me. I could hear his footsteps echoing on the marble floors of the vestibule as he pushed his way to the front doors where I was reluctantly shaking hands with our pastor.

Nick and I talked for about an hour, trying to fit 10 years into sixty minutes. He was also getting divorced so we had lots of horror stories to share and compare. It wasn't until Father Mark returned to lock the church doors that we realized we were alone on the sidewalk. Nick suggested we go to dinner the next evening to continue catching up. I agreed.

Funny how life works. Nick was a good looking guy with a great sense of humor. He also had a reputation for being a thief of hearts, but since I wasn't looking for love, I felt I was safe. When he picked me up the next night, he asked if I would mind if we stopped at his doctor's office. In those days, doctors still had evening hours to accommodate their working patients.

We couldn't have been in the waiting room more than five minutes when the inside door opened and in walked Mitch. One glance and I lost my heart. He was the epitome of every girl's dream—tall, dark, handsome, polished, well-mannered, well-spoken and a smile that could melt an iceberg. I knew immediately that he was the real deal and not some imposter who would use his looks and position to add notches to his bedpost. Unfortunately, he was also Nick's best friend and, even more unfortunately, he was in a relationship.

The quiet dinner for two became a laugh riot evening for three when Mitch joined us. I remember thinking, 'Why can't I meet a guy like this?' When I got home, I expressed those same sentiments to my mother, who offered this very profound statement, 'If you want something badly enough, you'll get it.' Considering that I had also wanted Brad...

Anyway, Nick and I and Mitch and Joanne began double dating, but it always seemed that Mitch and I talked more to each other than to our own dates. Since Mitch taught at the New York Institute of Technology three days a week, he began driving me to my office in Manhattan. Sometimes, if his schedule allowed, he would meet me for lunch. At one of those lunches, Mitch ordered a grilled cheese sandwich and slathered it with maple syrup. I thought it was disgusting. He still likes them that way but I no longer gag when he eats them. Now, I think they're wonderful because they bring back memories of new love.

Mitch and I kept our relationship strictly friends but as time passed, my initial infatuation with Nick began to wane. The more I got to know him, the more I realized he hadn't moved much past the eighth grade mentality. One evening, the four of us attended a civic fundraiser together. We had a great time and, as the night drew to a close, Joanne and I headed off to the bathroom for that one last "go" before the car ride home. While freshening our makeup, she put her hand on my arm and confided, 'I'm probably crazy to say this, but you and Mitch belong together. Our relationship isn't what it used to be, so if he should ask you out, don't be a fool. Go.' The moment was surreal. I remember a guilty feeling washing over me... the kind you might get if caught reading a stranger's diary.

Well, Mitch did ask me out, and I did accept, and the rest is history. Forty two anniversaries, two kids, five houses and more pets than the Bronx zoo, he remains the center of my universe. When my children ask how it is that we've remained in love all these years, I always tell them, 'You don't have to love somebody to like them, but you do have to like somebody to love them.'

Mitch is not only my best friend and confidante, he's the shoulder I lean on, the ear to listen, and the arms that hold me when I'm happy or sad. He has no hang ups about male/female roles, so he is equally comfortable with a dust rag and a hammer. On top of that, he makes a mean pasta primavera. What more could I ask for?"

"That's one hell of a story." Claudia could not help but to feel a touch of envy. She hid it under a smile of encouragement. "After you married Mitch, you never had any contact with Brad?"

"Not directly. I was pregnant with our son when Mitch got a phone call at his office. A man, who introduced himself as a lawyer for a major credit card company, asked Mitch if he was married to the former Diana McDonald. Mitch did not want to say anything that could cause me trouble so he asked for a phone number and said he would have me call back. When I did, the lawyer told me that the company had credit card applications with my signature as co-applicant. He explained that Brad had defaulted on the payments and I was now responsible."

"How could that be? You were already married a few years to Mitch."

"Exactly. I asked what name was on the applications. Brad had signed them Diana McDonald. Not only wasn't I Diana McDonald at the time they were filed, I had already taken back my maiden name and within a few months had married Mitch. The lawyer was very understanding. He asked for a copy of my divorce decree and that was the last I heard from him."

"Good lord. Your life is a perpetual nightmare, at least where Brad is concerned."

"I'm not unique. Almost all women who have been in abusive relationships continue to be victimized by their former spouses or boyfriends. It was Mitch who suggested I write *Private Hell* as a way of informing the public and purging those nightmares you mentioned. You see, while your reference was metaphorical, I do still have very real, very terrifying dreams. In them, Brad is sleeping beside me. When I see him, I start to scream at the top of my lungs. Mitch tells me that the sound is akin to very bad opera. I wake up feeling like I was trapped in a D-rated horror movie."

"You said on the phone that you're hoping this book will help other women?"

"I'm hoping this book will force society to give more than lip service to the problem of domestic abuse. 'An ounce of prevention…,' as Ben Franklin advised us. Far too many abused women have learned the painful truth that a *cure* is rarely possible."

"And the fact that you believe your former husband has returned to take his revenge gives credence to that statement. How can I help?"

"Tell me how to protect myself. The police refuse to intervene. The detective I spoke to told me that 14 in every 1,000 people are victims of stalking annually but that it's a crime that is difficult to prove and even harder to prosecute. It was obvious that the detective felt sympathetic but his hands were tied."

***

The launch party for *Private Hell* was held in the Legacy Place Barnes and Noble in Palm Beach Gardens, Florida. Because Diana Ciccone was a local resident and had something of a high profile in the community, the turnout was better than expected. As a first time author, having a named publisher accept her manuscript was a major coup. Getting it into a store like Barnes and Noble... Diana's feet were definitely not touching hard ground.

Knowing that both her publisher and Barnes and Noble were already planning a book tour kept Diana's knees knocking in time to the bullet train beat of her heart. She believed herself to be an excellent writer but almost overnight she had become an "author," and the difference in those titles was a mix of joy and fear. The pressure to succeed was on.

The second book signing was hosted by Another Broken Egg Café at Harbourside Place in Jupiter. Harbourside is the beautiful shopping and entertainment complex located just a few miles north of Diana's home. The turnout was far beyond expectations, and Diana couldn't help but laugh and wonder if it was the appeal of her book or the free beignets and coffee which the restaurant provided that had attendees hungering to meet her. Regardless, many fans stood on line to receive an autographed copy of *Private Hell*, and by day's end, Diana felt "baptized" into the exclusive circle of recognized journalists and authors.

The next book signing took place at the Barnes & Noble on Route 17 South in Paramus, New Jersey. Diana was going home and, although she did not fear returning to the scene of the crime, she was apprehensive about the possibility of seeing Brad again. Paramus was only 19 miles from Hoboken—Brad's place of residence and nightmare central for her. The abuse Diana suffered while living in the birthplace of Frank Sinatra always caused her to shiver whenever the singer was mentioned. She could not separate Ol' Blue Eyes from her painful past. Hence, she was not a fan.

The book tour took three months—too long for Mitch to be away from his medical practice. With no other recourse, Diana traveled alone. Besides New Jersey, she signed copies of *Private Hell* in book stores in Manhattan, Los Angeles, Chicago, Washington, D.C. and Connecticut. She spoke at luncheons sponsored by victims' rights groups and professional women's organizations. Her publicist did a great job of getting the word out, and the line of people waiting to meet her was always female heavy with a large number of those women bearing the physical and emotional scars of domestic abuse. Diana felt privileged to shake their hands and was honored to be embraced by the sisterhood that was taking root through her story.

Although the fictional account of revenge revealed in *Private Hell* gave readers chills, it was the personal letter from Diana at the front of the book that spoke to young and old, married and single women alike. Diana made it clear that she never seriously considered hurting herself nor had she actually contemplated murder. In fact, just the opposite was true. She believed with all her heart that women were much stronger than they realized. She was adamant that women could change the world if they put their minds to it. And she never used the word victim. They were all survivors. Her motto "Once Victimized – Now Victorious" was printed in bold letters on her business cards.

Diana's website—feelnoshame.org—provided resources and inspirational messages for women and men alike. She was only too aware of the devastating statistics presented by The National Coalition Against Domestic Violence. According to the NCADV, thousands of protective orders were issued every year and more than half of them were violated. Three women were killed every day due to domestic violence in the United States.

Every year 1.5 million women were physically assaulted by a partner or spouse and stalking affected over three million adults annually in the U.S. While the numbers were mind boggling, there was hope. Behind those figures were other figures... bodies – real bodies of real women who were reaching out to help others in need. These were the women who waited patiently to meet Diana and have her sign their copies of *Private Hell*.

"When I read your book...," one woman told Diana, "... I thought 'If she got out, I can get out.' I called my local Office of Victim Services and the help they provided has given me back my life. Thank you."

Diana was a huge supporter of using Global Positioning Satellites (GPS) for the prevention of domestic abuse and sexual assault. She had been shocked to learn how few cities and states used the systems. Part of the problem, she knew, was that each manufacturer offered systems with varying levels of protection and different interpretations of tracking and monitoring—the two common terms used to define GPS. These differences made purchasing systems confusing for municipalities with limited budgets. Many companies advertised that their control centers were staffed 24 hours a day, seven days a week, 365 days a year and, technically, that was true. There was, however, a caveat not as readily offered. Tracking merely allowed a probation officer to see where an offender was when a warning message was sent to his email account—not where that offender was at the present moment. An hour or more might pass before that warning was retrieved and, by then, the offender may already have committed another crime. Monitoring was done in real time meaning an offender was never out of sight.

When talking about the benefits of Global Positioning Satellites, Diana often referenced a story from when her children were small.

"Every morning began with complaints from my then five-year-old daughter that her eight-year-old brother was staring at her. My son, ever the nudge, would position a box of cereal between himself and his sister and pretend to read, while actually making faces at her. My daughter would grow more and more frustrated as her attempts to push the box away failed and the whining began. 'He's looking at me. He's looking at me.'

Now, in the context of satellite surveillance of sexual predators and domestic abusers, my daughter's words are music to my ears. We're looking at you. We're looking at you. At least, we should be."

Diana always closed by saying, "Please, don't forget. Any warning that is less than immediate is 59 minutes too late!"

Back home in Florida, Diana's calendar, while still heavy with personal appearances, finally allowed time to put her feet up or, better still, spend time with her grandchildren. She was just beginning to breathe a sigh of relief that the initial hoopla was over when the notes and gifts began to appear on her doorstep.

The first sign of trouble was a business size envelope left in the mailbox. It was typed and addressed with only Diana's first and last name. No return address. No stamp. No postmark. Inside was a message, also typed, on a plain white sheet of copy paper.

DMD: Interesting book

There was no signature but Diana knew it was from Brad. His surname—her surname when she was married to him—was McDonald not Douglas as she had used in *Private Hell*. During their marriage, Brad had often left Diana notes addressed DMD, which he claimed meant *Diana, my darling*. Diana decided not to tell Mitch. She hid the note in her dresser, refusing to believe that she was in danger. She hoped that by ignoring Brad's attempt at communication, he would go away.

A few weeks later, the photographs arrived. Diana would find them in unexpected places—scotch taped to the garage door, wedged in a bathroom window frame, nailed to a tree in her backyard... one or two a week. Each had been taken at a signing or an event she had attended while on tour. Diana was furious. She thought she had taken every precaution... had watched the crowds so carefully. Somehow Brad had skillfully hidden in plain sight.

Shortly after the photographs appeared, the drive-bys began. Around and around the block a car would go always following the same circuitous route and always slowing down as it passed the Ciccone house. Diana was unaware of it until a neighbor asked if she had noticed a stranger in their community. The neighbor thought it was a fan hoping to get an autograph. She mentioned that sometimes she would see the car parked a few blocks away, but it was always empty. It became routine for the neighbor to look for the car when she walked her dog. Diana watched and waited as well but just as suddenly as the car had appeared, it disappeared. She and the neighbor chalked it up to Jehovah's Witnesses or people soliciting money.

Once again, Diana relaxed only to be awakened by her car alarm blaring at 3:00 am. Some mornings, she awoke to find the doors on her minivan unlocked, the driver's seat moved, the mirrors readjusted and the radio stations changed. She began parking in the garage at night—a wasted effort. The side door leading from the garden to the garage was found open time and again.

Flowers followed... bouquets that were half dead and looked as if they had been stolen from a cemetery. Usually these were left on her patio table and Diana would toss them before Mitch came home. The day she found a vase filled with wilting lilies on the kitchen counter, she knew she had to take her head out of the sand. That was also the day she found that someone had used her toothbrush and left the remains of toothpaste splattered all over the sink and mirror in her bathroom. She and Mitch went to the police—another useless effort if ever there was one.

"The worst was yesterday," Diana told Allerd. "I haven't been able to sleep so, before the sun came up, I was standing at the living room window staring into space. Suddenly, that empty space was filled with a face. I had only the light from the moon, which wasn't very bright, to see it by, but I'm sure it was Brad. It was gone in a blink. Later in the day, I found a dead rat on our doorstep. A wire noose had been tied around its neck. The other end was tied to a shrub. The rat's head was nearly severed from struggling to escape. Message received."

"We'll hire a bodyguard and I'll put a private investigator on the case," Claudia Allerd reached for her phone. "The police will listen now or I'll be the one making the threats."

***

Diana and Claudia had numerous meetings with Angus Caruthers, the private investigator hired by Allerd. Angus was not the typical movie version of a Scotsman. His hair was more blonde than red and his eyes, although blue when wearing his favorite tee shirt depicting the Scottish flag, tended toward hazel.

Taller than six foot by about 4 inches, his shoulders were broad on a slender frame. Angus was a practical man, forthright in his manner of speech, honest to a fault, polite, friendly, yet, reserved. He was also stubborn and fearless—traits which some-times manifested by taking foolish chances. Having grown up in a world of violence, Angus Caruthers was a keen observer of human nature. Raised poor, if not poverty stricken, as a young boy he turned the front stoop of his tenement apartment building in Michigan into a window on the world. Early on, he realized that nothing in life happened by chance. There were always ob-servable signs if people were only willing to look for them. He enthusiastically shared examples of his youthful observations with his employer and her new client.

If Mrs. Acheson marched across Aberdeen Avenue with her pocketbook strap clenched in her fist like a baton, eight-year-old Angus knew that her son and daughter would suffer the ugly consequences of her bad day before going to bed that evening. The morning after Mr. Brodie teetered down the street singing *Scots Wha Hae*, Mrs. Brodie would have a black eye. If Mr. and Mrs. Hameldon were flush with money for cigarettes and whis-key, their son Ailean, Angus' best friend, would eat dinner at the Caruthers' table. Otherwise, he would go hungry.

Unlike his reticent ancestors, Angus could be downright

chatty once he got to know someone and felt comfortable in their presence. He adored Claudia, which meant that conversation was never in short supply when they were together. The moment he shook Diana Ciccone's hand, he knew he had found a kindred spirit.

The hard lessons Angus Caruthers learned in childhood became his motivation for choosing a career first as a police officer with a degree in criminal psychology and, now, as a private detective. Protecting others by predicting and preventing violence was a driving force in his life. Wanting Diana to fully understand the potential danger she was facing, Angus spent many afternoons educating her on the stalker mentality. He was a veritable encyclopedia... a rich source of information which allowed Diana to grasp how her once quiet life had become a maelstrom.

The writer in her welcomed the knowledge she was acquiring. Angus had done her research for her. On a personal level, what she was learning was very unsettling. She shared with Angus and Claudia a quote she read by David Foster Wallace.

"The thing about people who are truly and malignantly crazy: their real genius is for making the people around them think they themselves are crazy."

Angus was born to the podium. When he spoke, his deep voice held his audience with rapt attention, and Diana was no exception. Stalkers, she learned, could be either male or female. They crossed all boundaries. Some were introverts and some were extroverts but almost all were fueled by some degree of mental illness. The reasons for their actions were as numerous as the grains of sand on the beach and fear was always a part of their arsenal.

Some stalkers chose victims with whom they had had a previous sexual relationship. Some became fixated on public figures - a person they had never met but who they believed had been their intimate partner.

"When a stalker feels rejected..." Angus said, "...he or she usually hopes to exact revenge for actual or imagined damage to their self-esteem. On the surface, they can appear ambivalent about a breakup while underneath they are seething with resentment."

Angus also explained that many stalkers harbor feelings of resentment, believing that they have been mistreated. In their minds, the whole world knows of their humiliation. They usually have a desire to even the playing field and, by creating havoc in their victim's life, they achieve a false sense of power. There are stalkers who, out of a desire for friendship, attempt to establish an emotional connection to people with whom they have minimal contact. If the object of their attention offers the barest of encouragement... a smile, a nod... they see it as confirmation that their overtures are welcomed.

Diana repeated everything Angus said to her husband. So charged was she whenever she returned from a meeting that Mitch claimed his fingers tingled with electricity when he touched her. Diana's anxiety levels were high, and it was almost impossible for her to sit still. "Most stalkers...," Diana explained to Mitch, "... are indifferent to the stress they cause their prey. Mental illness often presents as delusional beliefs that the person they are stalking shares their feelings. The worst is the predatory stalker who seeks sexual gratification. These are usually males who become obsessed with a female stranger. The stalking may include voyeurism and deviant sexual practices. It can result in physical harm and death. My skin crawls just thinking that Brad could be outside watching."

Angus informed Diana and Claudia that, in his opinion, Brad fell into two categories. His actions mirrored those of both a rejected and a resentful stalker. Along with giving Diana information which could keep her safe, Angus suggested she keep a stalking journal in which she was to write down anything out of the ordinary that happened. He prepared a risk profile for her detailing not only the probability of physical violence but, also, the expectation of persistent and recurrent behavior. Diana was quite vocal that, in her opinion, the profile was a waste of Angus' valuable time. She already knew that Brad was persistent and she had been victimized by his violent recurrent behavior many, many times in the past.

Like most stalking victims, Diana originally convinced herself that her imagination was playing tricks on her. She feared over-reacting and looking like a fool if her suspicions were unfounded. She was also filled with self-recrimination and in denial that Brad was capable of such behavior. This was in direct conflict with what she knew to be true.

Angus knew only too well that the fear of looking like a fool could put people in a great deal of danger. He told Diana and Claudia of a personal experience which had happened three days after the bombing of the World Trade Center.

"My wife and I were visiting my sister and her family in Goodyear, Arizona. Goodyear is five miles south of Luke Air Force Base and 35 miles from Palo Verde Nuclear Generating Station, the largest nuclear power plant in the United States. My sister's son-in-law works in that plant. Shortly after arriving at our hotel, my wife and I went down to the lobby in search of sundries we had failed to pack. Near the elevator was a bank of pay phones and speaking heatedly on one of them was a man whose obvious anger drew our attention and that of all people standing nearby. Having a number of friends from the Middle East, I recognized his accent and a few random words although not the country of origin.

As we waited for the elevator to chime its arrival, I grew more and more uncomfortable. I nudged my wife and tilted my head in the speaker's direction. The gentleman's ire was growing and the words *Palo Verde* and *nuclear* kept surfacing in his conversation. My wife just shrugged her shoulders. Although she's well-versed in why I react as I do in certain situations, she thought I was making a big deal out of nothing. We went back to our room, but I could not silence the warning bells in my head. I returned to the public area and, under the phone the man had been using, found a piece of paper with an international number.

I called my office and a staff member tracked the number to

Afghanistan. I immediately called a contact at the Phoenix FBI office. You may remember that immediately after the attack, Americans were asked to report any suspicious actions to the authorities, so I did. Mine was the only phone call received from the hotel that day although everyone standing in the lobby had heard the same conversation I heard.

Did I overreact? I don't think so. Up until 9/11, we were a smug nation, thinking no one would dare to attack us. We are wiser now and with that knowledge comes the obligation to protect our homeland and the freedoms we hold so dear. We are all soldiers in the fight against terrorism."

"But, Angus..." Diana struggled to put her thoughts into words. "You're an expert on violence. I can understand why you reacted as you did. The rest of us... we can't spend our lives living in fear. That's no life at all."

"I don't want you to live your life in fear. I want you to live your life in conscious awareness. Think back to the Boston Marathon. Immediately following that horrific event, just about every journalist of any renown wrote an article in which they encouraged us to return to our normal lives. This, they believed, would be a slap in the face to terrorists... a message that they cannot destroy our freedoms. I have never forgotten the editorial written by Thomas L. Friedman for the New York Times. "This is our house," he wrote. "We intend to relax here. And we are not afraid."

I was happy that Mr. Friedman wasn't afraid, but I was furious that he was encouraging others to follow his erroneous thinking. He did the populace a disservice by suggesting that the rest of us embrace his mindset. Fear, when harnessed properly, can be an advantage.

Perhaps, our difference of opinion lies in our definitions of the word fear. To me, fear is our inner warning system, also known as gut instinct. It keeps us on our toes and heightens our senses. It protects us when we least expect to need protection. Fear also makes us deeply aware of the fragility of life. To quote

Benjamin Disraeli, 'Fear makes us feel our humanity.'

Never would I advocate that we let fear of the past prevent us from making decisions that enhance our present and future. However, the past is like a box of crayons. The application of its many colors, such as success, failure, peace, war, birth and death, give depth to our vision of life and liberty. Those colors can only benefit us as we move into an uncertain future. To ignore that fear has a place in our lives is to ignore that danger is all around us. Rather than professing that we are not afraid, let's acknowledge that we are and rightly so. Then, let's choose to temper our fear with the softer shades of awareness.

Do not ignore fear because doing so would allow our enemies to sneak up from behind and color over our lives and our country with their own brand of crayons. The color they will use is the deepest, darkest black of death and destruction.

Anyone unwilling to take responsibility for his or her own safety is a fool. The world we live in today is seriously void of human compassion. Personal agendas far outweigh concern for the masses. Whether it is an aggressive driver on the highway who thinks rage is his right, the neighbor who allows their dog to defecate on your lawn and shows no inclination to clean it up, a foreigner who does not agree with our liberties, or an ex-husband who harbors resentments for imagined transgressions, we need to accept that being victimized – by gun, knife, bomb or bully – is the way of the world.

Ignorance is not bliss, Diana. In fact, ignorance can be life threatening. Brad is the devil you know not one you don't know. He hasn't changed. You must take these threats very seriously."

***

Two months passed without any further signs of trouble. Diana believed that the investigation conducted by Angus and his surveillance team—with its strong potential for arrest and prosecution—had finally forced Brad to retreat. Once more, she felt safe enough to resume her daily exercise program. Early one morning, she decided to go for a bike ride, a pleasure she had completely abandoned since the book tour. Her latest novel, *Silk Suit/Stone Heart*, was nearing completion. The house was clean. The garden was raked. She had even had time to bake Nonna's famous apple pie. She felt hopeful and at peace.

Entering the garage through the laundry room, Diana was surprised to find the door already up and a woman standing next to Mitch's workbench. She was bent over with her back to Diana and gave the appearance of someone looking for a tool – a screwdriver, a hammer - something. Diana's surprised, "Oh!" caused the woman to turn around. Fleetingly, her mind registered that the woman was pretty, thin, had long dark hair and a somewhat ethnic appearance. Their eyes met and the woman smiled, but her smile was far from reassuring. The knife in her hand confirmed Diana's worst fears.

"Get out of my house!"

The stranger merely stared.

"Who are you?" Diana demanded.

"I am sorely tempted to say 'Your worst nightmare,' but melodrama has never been a strong suit of mine." By comparison to Diana's voice, which had screeched with terror, the woman's voice was almost lilting.

"How did you get in here?"

"Car doors are easy to unlock once you know how. I took the extra garage opener from your glove box months ago."

"You're the one who's been breaking into my car? Why? What do you want?"

"I would think the answer to that question is more than obvious." The woman dangled the knife for Diana to see.

"I'm going to call the police."

"No. You're not. You can try, but you'll only hasten the inevitable outcome of this meeting."

"Which is?"

"Your death."

"Who, the hell, are you?"

"I'm disappointed you don't recognize me. I'm your unlucky replacement. I'm who you would be had you not broken free of Brad. I envy you. Breaking free wasn't an option for me until recently. Thanks to you, I've found my way out.

"You're Brad's wife?"

"I'm Brad's possession... his prisoner."

"If I'm the reason you can finally... what was it you said... 'break free' why do you want to hurt me? Shouldn't you be grateful to me?"

"I am grateful to you. Very grateful. Reading your book was the smartest decision I ever made. When I reached the end, I felt as though I had been keep in a cage for a very long time and, suddenly, I realized there was no lock on the door. There was, however, a ferocious guard dog. Freedom required only that I kill the creature."

"I don't understand. How could you have known that I'm Brad's ex-wife?"

"The pen name you chose... I was barely half way into your story when I realized that Marjorie Markel, Diana Ciccone and the former Diana McDonald were one and the same person. The internet provided all the confirmation I needed."

"Even if you were able to fine my real name, none of my bios mention my past marital status."

"You poor, deluded woman. There are no secrets from the internet. Any and all information is available for a price."

"But you had no reason to connect me with Brad."

"Really? You thought 'Out of sight. Out of mind?' Brad has spent the last 40 years berating himself one minute for the way he treated you and cursing you the next minute for being a no good bitch. I've heard your name ad nauseum. Once, I actually dared to point out that the way he treated you was the way he treated me. No one needs to kick me in the face more than once. I'm a quick learner. I kept my mouth shut after that because unlike you, I didn't have anywhere to run. My parents feared Brad would kill me if they interfered. The feared he would kill me if they didn't. Their indecision was just as life threatening as Brad's fists."

Diana took a deep breath. Her voice and demeanor took on an element of calm and concern for her assailant. "What's your name?"

"Abha."

"I'm sorry you've suffered, Abha."

"Save your apologies. They won't change my mind."

"What has my book got to do with you plotting to kill me?"

"Once I read the vivid account of your marriage to Brad, which painfully and accurately mimicked my own life, I knew I could use your cowardly solution to my advantage. Unlike your Palma character, I have no desire to kill myself but killing him… that is very appealing. The problem with killing him is that I'll go to jail even though the killing will be justified. Prison doesn't appeal to me. I've been kept in a cage far too long. After considering numerous escape plans, I decided it would be much better if Brad killed you. Then, he'd go to jail, and I could get a divorce. Revenge is sweet."

"If you want a divorce, get a divorce. Why do you have to kill anyone? What's any of this got to do with Brad stalking me."

"Brad wasn't stalking you, Diana. I was."

"But I saw him."

"Yes... because he was following me. I told him I was going on business trips for my father, who is an importer of fine hand woven rugs. I've been his buyer since I was in my early twenties. Traveling is a constant for me. I knew if I was vague about where I was going and who I would be with... if I planted just a few seeds of doubt... Brad would immediately assume I had a lover. He would follow my trail of bread crumbs like a bird in a ravaged land, hoping to catch me in the act. While he was here in Florida looking for me, I was thousands of miles and a few continents away. I carefully planned every one of his steps along the journey... turned it into a scavenger hunt... and made sure your paths never actually crossed... at least, not up close and personal."

"That must have taken a tremendous amount of... of... deviousness. I'm not sure whether to fear you or admire you."

"I'll take that as a compliment. I have enjoyed tormenting you, but your private investigator, Angus Caruthers, is very good at his job. I believe he has discovered the truth. There's no time left to waste. If this were a game of chess, I would be forced to sacrifice my queen."

"Brad wasn't stalking me?"

"I hate it when people repeat my words back to me. Pay attention. No, he wasn't. He was stalking me, and I was stalking you pretending to be Brad. Brilliant... don't you agree?"

"Insane is more like it. How do you intend to convince him to kill me?"

"I don't intend to convince him to do anything. I'm going to kill you, and Brad will be blamed. I've set the stage perfectly. The notes... the flowers... the photographs... breaking into your house and car... that was all part of my plan. This knife... Brad's fingerprints are all over it and just for good measure, I've even brought along some hair clippings. After I stab you, I'll plant them on your body. Brad will be arrested, tried and found guilty and, if I'm really lucky, he'll get the death penalty rather than life in prison. All the pieces will fall neatly into place."

"Why? What have I ever done to you?"

"What a stupid woman you are! You didn't kill him when you had the chance. I know all about his fear of being poisoned and how he switches the plates before a meal. He's made me sample his food almost since day one of our marriage. I've hated you ever since I read your book. If you had poisoned him like you wrote in your story, I wouldn't be standing here now."

"I'm so sorry."

"Shut up. No one cares... not you, not God. I prayed—oh, how I prayed—but God either wasn't listening or he just didn't care. You have no idea how much Brad enjoys those nightly rape and torture sessions. His technique has improved immensely since you were last face down in a pillow."

"I can help you get free of Brad. Keep you safe. There are people... lots of people... who will give you a new start in life."

"It's too late for that. Plus, I've grown to like the idea of getting justice for myself."

"Abha, I understand that you want to make someone else suffer for the way you have suffered, but that won't change the past. With all the violence in the world, women should not be abusing women."

"Your mother abused you."

"Yes, she did, which is why I cannot understand why you

would want to hurt me. There is nothing to be gained from it."

"You never thought of punishing your mother?"

"No. Never."

"Gold star for you."

"Please. Listen to me. Despite being portrayed as the weaker sex, we women are strong in the most important of ways. Our perspective on life and liberty is very different from men. We hold morals and ethics to a higher standard. We understand injustice because we have been victimized by it."

"Bravo! Is that something from one of your books? If not for this knife in my hand, I'd actually clap."

"You won't get away with this. The police are on their way."

Smiling sadistically, Abha McDonald began to walk toward Diana, the knife held high and threateningly. With the agility of a cat, Angus stepped out from the kitchen doorway and blocked her progress. With one hand, he pushed Diana out of the way. The gun in his other hand added a visual exclamation mark to his demand for Abha to put down her knife.

Angus' sudden appearance stopped Abha's advance. There was confusion in her face... confusion that bordered on madness.

"I underestimated you. You knew I was coming. How did you know I would be here today?"

"While you were watching Diana, the police, with some help from my investigators, were watching you. We've known Brad wasn't involved for some time. Did you think we wouldn't contact him?"

"You didn't contact him. I monitored his calls. You never talked to him. You never met with him. I would have known."

Abha McDonald turned to Diana and spoke with a hatred so deep, it was bone chilling. "I put a GPS device on your car. There's a voice transmitter under your dashboard. I know everything about you!"

"Perhaps, but we knew about you as well. I never spoke directly to Brad but Angus did. So did the police in New Jersey. He has been helping them... helping us... for which I am very grateful."

Angus swept out his arm and moved Diana to safety behind him. Slowly, he advanced on Abha, steadying his gun with both hands as he walked. He never took his eyes off the knife now pointed at his stomach, not even as he responded to her ranting.

"We knew about the phone tracer and GPS, and we used them to our advantage. It's over, Abha. Put the knife down."

"I'm not afraid of you, Scotsman. You won't shoot me. I'm a woman. The headlines would turn it into another bad cop story."

"I'm not a cop." Taken at face value, Angus' words seemed unthreatening, but Abha recognized their not-so- hidden meaning. Bureaucracy would not hamper his efforts to protect Diana, and he wasn't the slightest bit worried about bad press.

Abha stood still and waited. Her breathing became shallow. Her heart pumped more slowly. She stared at Angus, gauging his strength and speed. He, in turn, watched the vein pulsing in her neck. He would know when she was ready to pounce and, if necessary, he would fire before she had taken one step.

"I've listened to every word you've spoken to Diana this morning," Angus warned Abha. "Taped the entire conversation. The police officers moving in behind you are also witnesses."

Abha hesitated, not sure whether to turn around and confirm that there were police officers behind her or call Angus' bluff. She decided on the bluff and a second order to put down her weapon was lost to the sound of gunfire as she charged Diana and Angus.

Angus Caruthers did not hesitate to fire his weapon. He was an expert marksman. The .38 caliber bullet from his revolver entered the soft, fleshy area just below Abha's shoulder, causing her to spin around and come face to face with personnel from the Palm Beach County Sheriff's Office waiting to arrest her. Being shot in the brachial plexus, the large nerve bundle which controls arm function, caused her to drop the knife. Although she was bleeding profusely from the subclavian artery, she still struggled as restraints were slipped over her arms and she was placed in a waiting ambulance. As the emergency vehicle pulled away, Claudia Allerd and Mitch Ciccone stepped out of the shadows where they had been monitoring events. Mitch wrapped his wife in an embrace while Claudia made some final notes in her iPad before speaking to Diana.

"I filmed it all. If escaping from Brad was that woman's goal, she succeeded. Prison bars will keep her safe from any further abuses… at least, those committed by her husband."

***

"Abha McDonald has been ordered confined to a mental hospital. She will undergo both cognitive behavioral therapy and psychodynamic therapy." Claudia filled the glasses of her guests, pouring from a bottle of 50 year old scotch.

"Psychodynamic therapy? I've never heard of such a treatment. What does it entail?"

"Psychodynamic may sound new age, Diana, but it has proven to be very successful in treating people who resort to violence when dealing with deeper emotions of aggression. The patient is encouraged to get in touch with their more vulnerable feelings like shame, humiliation and fear in the hope that, once they face these feelings, aggressive behavior will be curtailed."

"Do you think it will work for Abha?"

"I don't know, but the doctors told me it will be years before the possibility of her return to society will be considered."

Claudia sipped the whiskey; the burn in her throat slowly making its way through her body. "I have to say that's good news to me. I feel sorry for her but not enough to risk her hurting someone else."

"What about Brad?" Diana Ciccone was empathetic with all the second Mrs. McDonald had suffered. She hoped her ex-husband would be incarcerated for a long time so that Abha would get both peace and justice. She also hoped to avoid the possibility of a third Mrs. McDonald ever suffering a fate similar to Abha's and her own.

"Abha filed for divorce. Brad won't contest it. Her lawyer and the state's attorney made it clear that any attempt on his part to interfere with Abha's quest for freedom would be dealt with harshly. He's been ordered to stay away from her. If and when he sees the light of day, he will be wearing an ankle monitor. Perhaps, your desire to see GPS used more frequently to protect abused women will actually come to be the norm."

Mitch Ciccone looked doubtful. "How can you guarantee that he'll adhere to the court order?"

"Iron bars will make it easy for him to comply... at least, for the next 10 years. Under Jersey law, he is guilty of spousal rape, inflicting life-threatening injuries and serious bodily harm. He could have gotten 20 years but because he was cooperative with local police and my investigators, the prosecutor cut him some slack. I don't think he's being punished near enough, so with a little luck..." Angus' voice held not a trace of sympathy, "... he'll finally learn what it's like to be face down in a pillow while someone else violates his humanity."

Claudia Allerd picked up Diana's book and turned it around so that the cover was facing her guests. "My sources tell me that the other inmates wasted little time in showing Brad that hell on earth really does exist. He may have been deaf to Abha's prayers, but I'll bet 'God help me' is on Brad's lips nightly now."

Diana reached for her book and placed her finger over the black rose on the cover. "In 2010, I was asked to be an original oratory judge at a forensics competition held at Harvard. The teenagers who competed were among the brightest minds in the country. I was stunned by their ability to dissect and discuss complex and often controversial topics. One after the other, they spoke with a degree of intellect most adults would envy.

A young man of 16 or 17 held my attention with a speech entitled, *Does It Pay To Pray*. He began by quoting from the First Amendment...

Congress shall make no law respecting an establishment of religion, or prohibiting the free exercise thereof.

He used the quote to segue into a discussion on whether or not there should be a National Day of Prayer. The speaker informed the audience that U.S. District Judge Barbara Crabb had very recently passed a ruling echoing the sentiments of one of our Founding Fathers, Thomas Jefferson. I don't remember the rulings exact wording, but it was something to the effect that, because the nature of prayer was so intimate and capable of having a powerful effect on society, the government should not have the authority to influence a person's decision whether or not to pray.

Being a bit of an American History nut, I already knew that Jefferson was a deeply religious man. He, like Judge Crabb, believed that because religion was personal the government had no place passing directives or issuing opinions. After his election to the presidency, he discontinued the practice of proclaiming days of fasting and thanksgiving and was vilified for doing so. Despite the verbal pistol whipping he took, he remained staunch in his belief that church and state should forever be separated.

"I didn't know any of that."

"Most Americans don't, Angus. It's a sad statement on our

educational system. Getting back to the young man, he went on to state that, in his opinion, defining religion was not difficult. Prayer was the bigger challenge. He believed that most people would agree that prayer was a conversation with God—a display of devotion and a means of presenting petitions. By way of proof, he recited the church approved verse "Our Father, who art in heaven..."

At this point, many in the audience were nodding their heads in agreement. Then, he shocked them all by asking, 'But what about me—a non-believer?' I swear you could hear the air rush out of the room. A teenager declaring openly that he was an atheist? It was shocking.

Remember, I said that the these students were among the brightest minds in the country. Well, so bright was this mind that within minutes, he had everyone nodding in agreement again.

His counterpunch was not that he didn't believe in God but that he didn't believe it was God's responsibility to take care of mankind. It was our responsibility to take care of each other. For him, true prayer was the issuance of sincere wishes for the well-being of others—friends and strangers alike. When, in his heart, he felt the weight of troubles pressing down on someone in his social circle, he would think to himself, 'Please, help them.' The idea that God would work a miracle was, he said, '... the stuff of fairy tales.'

He went on to ask, 'So, who hears my plea?' You have no idea of the level of quiet in that room. Everyone was waiting for his answer, which was that he believed in the power of positive thought. He believed that it is possible to harness our minds to create a force field of healing energy. Actually, what he said was much more complicated but it would take an hour or more to explain his reasoning.

Was his thinking far- fetched? Maybe, but many times in my own life, I have been empowered just knowing that someone else cared about me. Throughout this entire ordeal, I've drawn tremendous strength from the kind wishes of family, friends and strangers. In fact, strangers' wishes have wielded more influence because I recognized that their offerings were not obligatory.

Think of all the people you know who are suffering from heartbreak, disease and depression. Each time you show them compassion... Each time you say, 'You are in my thoughts,' and each time you actually do think of that person, couldn't that be a prayer? If a burden is lightened even momentarily by an act of kindness, couldn't that be the fulfillment of prayer?

"This is very deep, Diana. What has it got to do with Brad?"

"Doctors have long felt that the fight against cancer is as much mental as medical. Words of encouragement such as 'I know you can do it' celebrate a victory in the making. Scientists believe that, when humans evolve to their full potential, they will have unimaginable power. Merely by melding our thoughts, we will have the ability to affect all matter. Maybe, we have that power already and don't realize it.

All day every day, we should be directing our thoughts and actions toward the positive. Believing that, as a society, we can and will do better and backing up that belief with good acts, is the first step. Even the smallest efforts, like a snowball rolling downhill, can have amazing results. When said with sincerity, 'I'm here for you' sounds prayer-like to me. At this point in my life, I've learned that there is much truth to the adage, 'Actions speak louder than words.' Prayer is only as good as the muscle we put behind it."

"And where is it that you are planning to put your muscle?"

"I want to help Abha. I don't know how, yet, but she needs to know that I don't blame her for what happened. It's a frightening thought that her life could have been my life."

"That's admirable." Claudia's smile was filled with admiration and encouragement. "If there is such a thing as life after death, you are going to be wearing a halo and wings."

"Don't get her started on the life after death thing. If you think the story you just heard was long, it's nothing compared to her ghost story."

"Ghost story? I love ghost stories!" Angus' face took on the excited expression of a kid at a campout. "Do tell."

"You asked for it." Diana smiled mischievously. "When Mitch and I met, my father had already been dead for some time. My mother kept no pictures of him in the house, and I had not even a wallet-sized photo to remember him by. Everything that was my father had been moved to the attic. My mother preferred not to be reminded of her part in his early passing.

My dad loved me. Of that I have no doubt. He was both father and mother in many ways. If I stubbed my toe, dad felt the pain. As you know, the years between my graduation from high school and my dad's death were traumatic. I've always believed that my marriage to Brad is what caused my father to suffer his fatal heart attack. There is no doubt in my mind that his constant worry about me hastened his demise.

There is also no doubt in my mind that my dad would have embraced Mitch as the son he never had. I'm positive about that because dad introduced himself to Mitch a few weeks after we were married. Yes, he was still dead, but Mitch saw him clear as day standing at the foot of our bed.

Mitch picked up the story.

"On the evening in question, I awoke needing to go to the bathroom. At the time, we lived in a tiny apartment. The master bedroom was miniscule; its smallness necessitating that our king sized bed be pushed almost to the wall on one side. It was easier for me to climb over Diana than to squeeze out on my side. Just as I got one knee over her sleeping torso, I saw a man standing a few feet away, smiling at me. I felt no fear. In fact, I felt... well, peaceful is the only way I can describe it.

Still on my knees, I asked, "What do you want?" The apparition didn't answer, but he did lift his hand in a two-finger salute. Then, he turned and walked away, slowly disappearing as he went. I looked at the clock on the nightstand. It was 2:00 am. I got up, went to the bathroom, returned to bed, and immediately fell into the most restful sleep I've ever had."

Diana, once again, took up the recitation.

"In the morning, Mitch told me the story. The hair on my arms literally stood up as he described my father—his mustache, haircut, stately nose, and he was wearing his favorite shirt. The two-finger salute... that was how my dad waved goodbye to everyone.

Of course, I was skeptical. Now, remember I said earlier that there were no photographs of my father. Mitch had never seen a picture of him. We immediately drove to my mother's house, where I tore the attic apart looking for old family albums. My dad and his two brothers looked so much alike they were often mistaken for triplets. I found those pictures. I also grabbed photos of other deceased male relatives just for comparison purposes. Back downstairs in the kitchen, I lined the photos up on the table and asked Mitch, 'Any of these guys?'"

Again, Mitch took over the storytelling.

"Yeah," I told her and pointed to one of the photographs.

"This man. This is the man I saw."

"I'm always leery about telling this story," Diana reached for Mitch's hand and held it tightly. "And judging from the looks on your faces, it's good that I am. Most people will say, 'Wow. That's amazing.' Their body language... sort of like your body language... says, 'This woman is nuts!' Nuts or not, I choose to believe. I know my dad is still looking out for me, and with Mitch as my husband, he no longer needs to worry. His two-finger salute was a sure sign of his approval.

Lots of people are afraid of ghosts, but I think of them as the continuation of the conscious mind. Can you imagine how much better the world would be if we were able to communicate with our past selves; to lasso and hold onto those rare moments of dé-jà vu that we all experience. What better teacher than our own mistakes?

Perhaps, the day will come when the human brain will evolve to its full potential. Wouldn't it be amazing to remember every-thing and have the power to change the world for the better with-out first having done harm?"

"What I don't believe is that you haven't worked that story into a novel yet." Claudia nodded with appreciation for Diana's story telling abilities. "I think there are a lot of people who feel as you do. Your ghost story would make the grieving process a lot less painful. What do you think, Angus?"

"I'll keep my ghosts at Disney's Haunted Mansion if you please. My English grandmother used to tell a story about a man from Birmingham who dreamed about a past life in the mid-1600s. In these dreams he saw himself in the body of another man working as a guard at the Scottish border. This man... the man in the dream not the man having the dream... was a foot sol-dier in Cromwell's army. My grandmother knew his name but I can't remember it now.

When the man having the dreams was hypnotized, he remem-bered more details and actual locations. He and his brother began to visit the places he remembered. Sometimes they would dig around and a few times they found small items that could be dated back to the 1600s. I remember my grandmother saying that the man... the dreamer... was able to give a detailed description of a church tower that had a yew tree growing out of it. Everyone was impressed because the church tower had been taken down in 1676 and there were no written records stating what it actually looked like. People had always believed the story of the tree to be mere folk lore.

Eventually, historians pressed for more and more details, but the man was not able to answer their questions to their satisfaction. The consensus became that the guy had not lived before but was merely dreaming about stories he had heard growing up."

"You didn't say whether you believe in life after death or not."

"Considering the kind of people I've met in my business, I hope that the dead stay dead and buried forever. A life of violence often leads to a violent life. By that I mean that men, women and children who are victimized, especially those who are victimized by the very people who are supposed to love and protect them, can find it difficult to control their frustration and anger. Rather than finding a non-destructive outlet as Diana did with writing *Private Hell*, they succumb to the need for revenge. Often, that revenge is directed at innocent people... those who are in no way responsible for the pain the avenger has suffered.

Many criminologists believe that, while there is a social and environmental element to violent behavior, biology is the strongest influence. We are born optimists or pessimists. Thus, we are pre-programmed to see the glass as half full or half empty. Optimists believe that something better lies ahead. No matter how heavy the weight on their shoulders, they can still lift themselves up and move forward. Pessimists see only deepening darkness, which leads to more pain and frustration. Where the optimist rises, the pessimist sinks. Therapy is only moderately successful. A bad brain is a bad brain and, unfortunately, we cannot remove the damaged parts and repair or replace them with something better.

Children raised by abusive parents often display violent tendencies as they age. Abha's father was a stern disciplinarian. Research has shown that children who have been inappropriately disciplined can and do develop mental problems. Abha loved her father, but she also feared him. When she married Brad, she merely continued the cycle of abuse, believing the treatment she received was deserved. Spending her early years under her father's thumb preconditioned her to expect and accept intolerable acts of violence.

Diana, let me ask you a question. Would you want Brad to return in another life? Would you want to set someone of his character lose upon more innocent women?"

"No. Of course, not. I just don't believe that the human race could possibility have advanced as quickly as it has unless some essence of who we are continues to exist. What if the hereafter is nothing more than a huge warehouse – like Sears – and our intellects are collected and redistributed to new souls? Maybe, sometimes, there's a glitch in the system and somebody gets too much of the good stuff or too much of the bad stuff. That could explain both child prodigies and serial killers."

"Well, it's certainly an interesting topic, one you should consider pursuing in your next book. I have to say that in all my years as an attorney I've never had a client as interesting as you. For now, let's just be grateful that two very troubled souls are no longer able to hurt innocent people."

A chorus of "Amen's" filled the room.

A Life Unlived

What is this life? Its purpose unclear
The road often broken and cobbled with tears
This path have I chosen or has it chosen me
Will I walk it alone or be accompanied.

Pain distorts my visage
Am I but a mirage
Invisible. Illusionary. Imagined
Gone.

Donna M. Carbone
2011

Through Thick and Thin...

is the first in the series of Cat Leigh and Marci Welles crime novels. Discover the who and why of the Kalendar Killer murders by touring the crime scenes with our two favorite homicide detectives.

Coming in December 2016

The second Cat Leigh and Marci Welles Crime Novel

SILK SUIT – STONE HEART
A Cat Leigh and Marci Welles Crime Novel

PROLOGUE

January 2009

Although the New Year was nearly two weeks gone, there remained a lingering sense of holiday cheer in the air. Wire candy canes covered in red and white plastic fringe still hung from street lights along PGA Boulevard in Palm Beach Gardens, while store windows festooned with green and gold garland announced a *LAST CHANCE* to buy after Christmas bargains.

For Homicide Detectives Cat Leigh and Marci Welles, this seasonally chilly Saturday evening was definitely a reason to celebrate. It was the partners first night off in nearly four months. They were exhausted from carrying a heavy case load and had been eagerly anticipating an evening out since the clocks had jumped ahead an hour the previous November. Quiet dinners in restaurants that did not require plastic utensils and styrofoam takeout containers were special occasions that usually happened only when the dusting of white powder on city streets was actual snow. Since the likelihood of that happening in south Florida was never, getting through an evening on the town without a call from the Palm Beach County Sheriffs' Office dispatcher was a miracle. Thus, it was with great surprise that Cat, Marci and their significant others found themselves seated in a secluded corner of the River House Restaurant in the Soverel Harbour Marina at 7:30 pm on Saturday, the 13th of January.

Cat, long blonde hair cascading to near her waist, was dressed in her usual fashionista style while Marci had exchanged her uniform—heavy rubber soled shoes and man tailored slacks and jacket—for stilettos and a Jones of New York black a-line dress bought on sale at TJ Maxx. The high heels were a necessity as, when not carrying a gun on her hips, her petite stature usually caused her to be overlooked in a crowd. Her short, dark hair encased her freckle-sprinkled face like filigree framing a cameo and, when seen in profile, her alabaster skin completed the illusion. More accustomed to being seen as zaftig rather than hubba hubba, she could not resist twirling around like a plastic ballerina atop a little girl's jewelry box as her dinner companions showered her with praise.

So startling was Marci's transformation from tough cop to wicked woman that Cat, her fiancé Kevin and Marci's husband, Ian, spent most of the meal toasting her new look. By the time they finished their steak and shrimp dinners, there were two empty bottles of Brunello di Montalcino on the table attesting to the expensive sincerity of their compliments.

"I've been trying to get you into a dress for years," Cat smiled her approval at her long-time best friend. "The last time I saw you in heels was senior prom. You didn't even wear heels to your wedding. You look amazing, Marci."

The two couples were practically giddy both from having imbibed a fair amount of fermented grapes and at having an uninterrupted couples night which did not require a diaper bag, squeaky toys and cheerios. Sonora Leslie, Marci's and Ian's 22-month-old daughter, was having a night out of her own—a sleepover at Grandma Nancy's house. So heady was the feeling of freedom that the couples decided to order dessert, coffee and after dinner drinks. That was their first mistake.

As they sipped their Sambuca-laced espressos, the conversation veered to a case Marci and Cat had recently investigated—a road rage incident that had turned into murder by Louisville Slugger. Since the suspect was in custody and the newspapers had his face and name plastered all over their front pages, the partners felt comfortable discussing the details of the crime.

As some of the more gruesome aspects were revealed, they remained oblivious to the less than thrilled looks being cast their way by Ian and Kevin.

According to Amarus Sanchez, the wife of the late Domingo Sanchez, she had sat petrified in the front passenger seat of the family's Dodge Ram pickup while Ricardo Ruiz stood on the hood of the truck and smashed the windshield. She had watched horrified, screaming until her voice was nothing more than a rasp, as her husband's head was bashed in. The sound of her terrified screams made their attacker laugh more manically with each swing of the bat.

Ruiz was no stranger to law enforcement in Florida. His rap sheet included being sentenced to seven years for firing 10 rounds at a Riviera Beach family during a holiday gathering in 2003. Jevon Wilson, the owner of the home where the shooting took place, told police that he had argued with Ruiz earlier in the day but, since they had settled their differences, he gave the altercation no further thought. Once the shooting began, it became obvious that Ruiz, who was a member of the Spanish Cobras gang, did not share Wilson's "It's over. Let's forget about it" mindset.

As the sun stroked with the horizon, Ruiz drove slowly past the house on Jog Road where Wilson's mother, wife and infant daughter were sitting on the front porch and opened fire. Whether intentional or not, the three family members were unharmed by the spray of bullets. Only a few cars were hit and the living room window shattered. Ruiz was quickly arrested but, since the only damage was to property, when found guilty of first degree assault and carrying a pistol without a permit, his sentence was reduced to three years. He served his time without incidence. No sooner was he back on the streets than he was back in trouble.

Domingo Sanchez was not as lucky as the three Wilson females. The detailed report given by his wife stated that the incident began when her husband cut Ruiz off while driving south on the I-95. "We had to get in front of him. He was veering from left to right, crossing into one lane and then the other. We were afraid to get caught behind him or to even be near him. Our exit was coming up, and we just wanted to get off the highway."

Mr. and Mrs. Sanchez lived in Delray Beach and, as they approached the Atlantic Avenue exit ramp, Ruiz caught up to them, honking his horn and giving them the finger. He drove threateningly close to the Sanchez's truck and threw a handful of change at the vehicle. Some of the coins sailed through the open window, hitting Domingo Sanchez in the eye.

Concerned that his sight had been impaired, Sanchez pulled over on the exit ramp. Ruiz also pulled over and, baseball bat in hand, walked back toward the pickup. Words flew and when it became obvious that Ruiz was out of control, Amarus Sanchez pleaded with her husband to get back in the truck, which he did. The next thing they knew, Ruiz was standing on the hood and swinging at the windshield with all his might. He did not stop until what was left of Mr. Sanchez's head hung to his chest, blood and brains covering the inside of the vehicle as well as Mrs. Sanchez's face and clothing.

"Truthfully," Ian Welles said to his wife, "this is not how I had hoped to end our evening. It doesn't seem to matter how long we are married or how often I read and hear about these crimes, they never get less disturbing. It's hard for me to believe that you and Cat can see such violence and not be affected by it, especially after the Kalendar Killer case. I don't think I will ever forget the horrible way those people died."

The Kalendar Killer case involved a series of five brutal murders over an eight month period in 2006. Each of the murders took place on a major holiday and each of the victims was found in a public place wrapped in a banner proclaiming "Happy" whatever special day was being observed. Solving the crimes had put Cat and Marci in the spotlight for nearly a year. Mother's Day, Father's Day, Independence Day, Labor Day, Halloween and Thanksgiving would never again be celebrated without members of the Palm Beach County Sheriff's Office and their families offering a moment a silence for the victims.

During the investigation, local media had described Cat and Marci as inept and then, after they had solved what had at first appeared to be an unsolvable mystery, as heroes. Neither title appealed to the detectives. Their job was to protect and serve. Nothing else mattered. Friends, family and co-workers knew that the one character trait they were most proud of was one they didn't have… ego.

"Ian, sweetie, I'm sorry we've upset you. For Cat and me… well, we've just gotten used to it. It isn't that we aren't bothered by the crimes. It's that we're no longer surprised by the brutality people inflict upon one another."

"I know and I admire the lengths to which the two of you go to keep this community safe, but let's talk about something else. Cat, I must compliment you on choosing this restaurant. The food was all you promised it would be."

"Thanks, Ian."

Cat squeezed Kevin's knee under the table as a silent apology should he, too, be disturbed by the conversation. "The River House has been a favorite of mine for a long time, not only because they have the best beef and seafood in the county but because seeing the waiters make Caesar salad the old-fashioned way reminds me of Easter Sunday dinners at my grandmother's restaurant in New Jersey. As a little girl, I loved 'the show' as I used to call it."

"I didn't know your grandmother owned a restaurant."

"La Vecchia Lanterna. I'm sure I told you, Marci, but I probably mentioned my Uncle Ducky."

"You did. I remember thinking that was a weird name for a grown man. How did he get it?"

"Uncle Ducky was really Uncle Donald. Seems he was a slow talker when he was a toddler. No amount of encouragement could get him to say Mama or Dada or baba… nothing. He was mute. By the time he was three, my grandparents were worried and frustrated. One day, they took Uncle Donald to the zoo and, as soon as he saw the ducks, he began to quack. From that moment on, he was Ducky."

"I'm assuming he did eventually speak."

"Of course. Actually started that very day. Full sentences and complex thoughts. You couldn't shut him up. Turned out he was gifted."

"And he ran the restaurant?"

"Let's just say he had his finger in a lot of enterprises, not all of them successful or legal. He was, however, a great chef and made a to-die-for Caesar salad dressing."

Marci, who hated just about every ingredient in a Caesar salad including the Romaine lettuce, did not share Cat's palate-pleasing enthusiasm for the recipe or the presentation. "If you could deep fry the green stuff, I'm sure I'd change my mind," was her usual retort whenever Cat mentioned healthy eating. She had a penchant for anything that could be plunged into boiling oil although she did draw the line at the cheeseburgers topped with a scoop of deep-fried cinnamon ice cream often served at the South Florida Fair. Those she considered, "Yucky!"

Whereas Cat enjoyed watching as the over-sized wooden bowls were rubbed with garlic cloves before being mashed with salt and anchovies, Marci preferred slathering her iceberg with ranch dressing spooned from a ten gallon jar. While Cat was watching the raw eggs being whisked with lemon juice, mustard, olive oil and parmesan cheese, Marci was holding her napkin to her face and pretending to gag. To Cat, a few extra anchovies and fresh ground pepper were the perfect finishing touches. To Marci, a pile of croutons the size of Mount Vesuvius added just the right crunch. The one thing they did agree on was that wine made everything taste better.

Cat had just licked the last bit of cannoli cream from her

dessert fork when a scream from a nearby table brought the evening to a sudden halt. Eileen Gardener, the wife of former Florida Governor Jon Everett Gardner, stood with her hands to her mouth staring down at her husband's body, which lay crumbled on the floor. Keeping Mrs. Gardner from collapsing in a faint was the Governor's Secretary of State, Alvin Langdon, and his wife, Tracy.

Governor Gardner had held office from 1971 to 1979. He was a career politician who, despite the passage of more than a half century of birthdays, had an encyclopedic memory for names and faces. Although it had been 40 years since he called the Governor's Mansion in Tallahassee home, he never missed an opportunity to shake a hand or pat someone on the back.

Upon entering the River House's main dining room, the Governor had immediately recognized Cat and Marci, who were something of minor celebrities since solving the Kalendar Killer murders. Before settling down to peruse the menu, he stopped to express his appreciation to his "... two favorite detectives" for their service to Palm Beach County and the State of Florida.

The cordialities over, Cat, Marci, Ian and Kevin turned their attention back to talk of personal matters and paid no more attention to the Gardeners and Langdons. Occasionally, when a burst of loud laughter pierced the air, Cat and Marci would look over and smile in appreciation of what was, obviously, a good time. The Governor had mentioned that he and "the Mrs." were celebrating 60 years of happy marriage. From the way Eileen Gardener hung on her husband's words and the way she affectionately stroked his arm, it was impossible to miss that the love light in her eyes was still shining brightly.

No sooner had the Governor swallowed his first forkful of salad than the frivolity turned to terror. Hysteria replaced happiness as he toppled to the floor, a foamy sputum forming on his lips.

Marci and Cat immediately rose and rushed to help. That was their second mistake of the night. Had they stayed in their seats, what followed would have become the responsibility of responding officers called to the scene by the house manager. However, Marci and Cat lived their lives by upholding their oath of service. They had pledged to put the public's needs before their private wants and desires and helping a former governor was a top priority. The effects of the wine dissipated in the few seconds it took them to get to their feet.

Marci got down on her knees to check for a pulse while Cat held out her badge and identified herself to the manager, who stood averting his eyes from the Governor's body. His legs were shaking so hard and fast that he resembled a dog with fleas. Barely could he string three words together to make a sentence. "He... dead... Is?"

Cat kept her voice low so as not to upset nearby patrons. "I don't know yet. We'll need to secure this area. Please have your staff block all exits to prevent anyone from leaving."

As the manager hurried away, Cat turned to the horrified diners. Most were gaping at the Governor's lifeless body as though expecting to see a reenactment of Lazarus rising from the dead.

"Ladies and gentlemen..." Cat kicked off her shoes and stood atop a chair to address the crowd. "The waiters will escort you to the lounge area. We know you have concerns. You are not in any danger. However, you may be witnesses to a crime and so must remain in the restaurant until a police officer has taken your statements. Please go quietly. Do not remove anything from your table except your personal belongings."

As the patrons filed out of the dining room, Marci rose from her knees and motioned to Cat that Governor Gardner was beyond saving. Her resuscitation efforts had failed. Together they turned to the very recent widow and expressed their sympathies.

"Mrs. Gardener, I'm Detective Marci Welles and this is my partner Detective Jessica Leigh. We are sorry for your loss. I assure you the Sheriff's Office will do everything it can to find out what happened here."

Eileen Gardener grabbed Marci's hand as she spoke. "Thank you, Detective. My husband... is there any..." Sobs replaced words as she sank into a chair supported by her friends.

Just then a loud banging was heard on the front door. Cat glanced in the direction of the lobby and saw the Homicide Department's superior officer—the gravel-voiced Captain Karen Constantine—motioning frantically to be let in. The Captain had a look of dark anger on her face as she pleaded with a waiter who was taking his job of sentinel a bit too seriously. Despite Captain Constantine repeatedly stating her name and rank in an ever increasing decibel, the waiter insisted on more identification than the gold shield pressed against the glass panel in the door.

Tall, imposing, often sullen, and sporting a scalp-baring Marine regulation haircut, Karen Constantine had eyes the color of charcoal briquettes after a long day of barbequing. Her unwavering dedication to upholding the law began before birth. Her father, a beat cop in the days when cops actually walked a beat, had had a miniature police uniform specially made for her to wear on the day she was brought home from the hospital.

The Captain wore her badge and gun with a degree of poise few top models possessed when sashaying down a runway. Recently appointed to head up the PBC Sheriff's Office murder and mayhem division, she was making many much needed, but not necessarily liked, changes. Those changes accounted for her nickname, Constantine the Hungarian, a not so flattering reference to the popular sword and sorcery comic book character, Conan the Barbarian.

Marci and Cat admired the Captain and, after being the two lone women in the homicide division for the past few years, were happy to have a superior who understood how hard it was to make it in a man's world. Since Captain Constantine had taken over, Marci and Cat rarely heard their macho-challenged counterparts whisper aspersions about women best serving the department on their backs or knees. So determined was Captain Constantine to avoid sexual harassment charges that she had verbally castrated a male officer her first day on the job after hearing him reference Cat's and Marci's physical appearance by calling them "Thick" and "Thin."

Constantine ruled her little corner of the world with an iron fist. Her voice was nothing if not authoritative. When she spoke, she sounded like a four-pack-a-day smoker although she had never taken so much as a puff in her life. Health conscience, the frown lines on her forehead deepened each time one of her subordinates entered the office followed by a low hanging cloud of nicotine. She cared deeply about the men and women in her charge but she'd be damned before she would allow herself to be seen as a softy. No one was fooled.

Finally having convinced the waiter that she was, indeed, the law, Captain Constantine strode across the dining room with long steps reminiscent of a cheetah stalking its prey. "What happened?" Her strident voice demanded answers from her two top detectives. "How did you get here so fast?"

"We were already here having dinner… sitting just two tables away." Marci hung her shield around her neck as she spoke. "We've put a call in for Doc Geschwer. I'm no expert but I'm certain the M.E. will confirm the Governor was poisoned."

The Captain stared at Marci, a quizzical look in her eyes. "I don't think I've ever seen you in a dress before, Detective."

"And you probably never will again. Nothing good ever comes from trying to be what you're not."

"I see it as just the opposite. Thanks to your evening out, you and Cat were on scene when this crime was committed. That means there's less chance of evidence being removed or tainted. I'd say fashion and fate played equal roles here tonight."

Once the crime scene was secured and all the witnesses had given their statements, Cat and Marci joined their significant others in the car for the short drive home. Everyone was tired, but Cat was chatty… the evening's crime having resurrected the memory of a similar event her parents had experienced years earlier.

"Did I ever tell you about the time my parents were out to dinner and a man died at the next table?"

A chorus of "No's" answered from the car's dark interior and, with encouragement from three now wide awake people, Cat told her story.

"In the town where my family lived before moving to Palm Beach County, there was a seafood restaurant called Harbor Lights. The food was outstanding, and the ambience was just the right blend of formal and casual. Not stuffy but definitely not a jeans and tee shirt kind of place.

Saturday nights usually found my parents at 'their' table. So often did they eat at Harbor Lights that they had taken to thinking of the secluded booth overlooking the gardens as their own. On this particular evening, they were enjoying a meal of Chateaubriand. As was customary, the meat was carved tableside with dramatic flair, and they were watching the waiter perform his magic when two elderly couples were given the table closest to them. My parents smiled; the new arrivals offered a pleasant 'Good Evening' before settling down to peruse the menus. Mom and dad continued sipping wine and talking, almost totally lost in a world of their own.

Every now and then, my parents would look around the room just to see what was happening and, in so doing, they noticed the progress of those four people. On some level, they were aware that courses were being delivered and that the couples were enjoying themselves. When they told us this story later in the evening, they said that during the early portion of the meal, the foursome seemed to be having a lively discussion, laughing and poking each other for emphasis. That all changed when their main courses were delivered to the table.

One of the gentlemen appeared to have fallen asleep in his chair. His head was tilted forward onto his chest and the position of his body made it difficult for the waiter to place his plate in front of him. Mom and dad overheard the waiter asking if everything was all right. 'Oh, yes,' the wife responded. 'He often does this. Not to worry.'

The waiter left the man's dinner and went off to see to his other customers. My dad, who had been watching for a few minutes, rose and approached the couples' table. He apologized for interrupting but said that he believed the man was in distress. He suggested they call for paramedics.

The wife assured my dad that her husband was fine. She said, 'He does this all the time.' Just as my father was about to walk away, the man's upper body fell forward onto the table. His face nearly landed in his dinner plate. No one seemed to care. The wife stood up and repositioned him in his seat so that he was sitting up straight. Then, she sat down and continued eating and talking with her friends.

My father was certain that everything was not fine. He knew there was a problem, but he was uncomfortable pressing total strangers to do his bidding. He motioned for the manager, who my parents knew personally, and explained his dilemma.

'I think that guy is dead,' my dad told the manager. 'You need to get him out of the restaurant before your patrons panic.'

The manager spoke with the wife, who gave consent to lift her husband's body while still seated in the chair and remove him from the table. The waiters assigned to this less than pleasant task earned an extra tip that night which my mom and dad graciously gave them. Paramedics were called, and the man was whisked away to the hospital. The wife and her friends continued to eat.

When they were through with their dinner and had paid their bill, the wife thanked my parents by saying, 'There was no reason to waste the food. My husband would want us to finish our meals.'

And, with that, they left.

Now, here's the best part. The man had died, but the paramedics revived him in the ambulance. Three weeks later, guess who was seated at that same table while mom and dad were having dinner. Thankfully, my parents were already on dessert when the couples arrived."

CHAPTER ONE

March 2010

With the nightly news hurling a barrage of criticism at a small percentage of bad cops while failing to recognize the thousands of police officers who unselfishly put their lives on the line every day to protect their communities, law enforcement throughout the country was taking a walking on eggshells approach to crime. Homicide Detectives Jessica "Cat" Leigh and Marcassy "Marci" Welles were all too familiar with negative publicity having received many a verbal slap in the face from the media during the Kalendar Killer investigation in 2006. They and their colleagues on the force had been preparing for an onslaught of disparaging press ever since Palm Beach County Sheriff Mike Brickshaw had gone on record saying he would support and defend his officers unless and until someone brought him proof of wrongdoing. Unfortunately, his stance only infuriated the minority communities whose members were often deliberate targets for racist cops. Brickshaw's assertions that there were "… good and bad people in every walk of life—doctors, lawyers, accountants, bankers, bakers, butchers… all people," did little to assuage the outrage that was manufactured by paid professional agitators in lower income neighborhoods.

With a long lineage of law enforcement professionals on her family tree, Cat took the slings and arrows personally. Her paternal grandfather had been a hard core investigator in one of the toughest cities in the country—Camden, New Jersey—at a time when organized crime ran the waterfront. For more than 25 years, her father had been a police physician in the northern New Jersey town of Fort Lee—gateway to Manhattan via the George Washington Bridge. Forty percent of her father's patients were in law enforcement. Another 40% were the criminals those police officers chased. The remaining 20% were just average folks. Almost all were of Italian descent. Day after day, week after week, these men sat in her father's waiting room. Some of them were friendly. Some were not. Some were funny. Others were best left alone. Tall, short, fat, skinny, tattooed and toupéed, each was unique in his own way, but the one thing they had in common was a deep dislike for honest labor and an intuitive sense of who to trust. God forbid you gave them reason to distrust you.

Cat had spent her teen years earning her way by running her father's home office. She got to know all the patients well… the good, the bad, the innocent, the guilty and the chameleons, of whom there were many.

Raised as a pure blooded Italian under the watchful eye of Nonna Zocchio, her maternal great grandmother, Cat's ancestry was more like the League of Nations. Her family tree included traces of Irish, German, English and Scottish. Nonna Zocchio was the matriarch of the family. She had been born in the northern capital of Trento, an Alpine city at the foot of the Dolomite Mountains, and immigrated to America as a young woman. Trento was the educational, scientific, financial and political center for the region. Her paternal great grandparents came from Rodi Garganico in southeastern Italy. Situated on the Adriatic Sea, Rodi was one of the most popular seaside resorts.

Valuing her Italian heritage as highly as she did, Cat was partial to men with dark hair and eyes. She was not repulsed by someone with a Caesar-esque nose provided the nose didn't enter a room before its owner. When she became engaged to the very blond, very Irish Kevin Kavanagh, the person most surprised was Cat herself. Marci swore that there was a gravitational pull which compelled Cat to hire only Italian doctors and Italian contractors. Her preference for Italian restaurants needed no explanation.

"Italians, like every ethnicity, feel more comfortable among their own kind," Cat said whenever Marci commented on the high percentage of burly Italians with unusual occupational titles Cat had met as a teen. There was The Hammer, Nick the

Knuckle, and the less fear-inducing in name only, Red Ritchie—Cat's first crush. Unlike the swarthy men who frequented La Vecchia Lanterna and her father's medical office, Ritchie was a carrot top, tall and thin with startling blue eyes in a handsome and, surprisingly, angelic looking face. Unfortunately, any further association with angels happened only in the hereafter.

Marci loved hearing Cat talk about her youth in New Jersey especially since growing up in West Virginia had been boring by comparison. Whereas Cat's family included some very edgy characters, Marci's grandparents, parents, siblings, aunts, uncles and cousins were a folksy lot who enjoyed simple pleasures. The most daring escapade she could remember from her youth was sneaking Mollie May, the neighbor's heifer, into McDonald's grocery story and hanging a sign around her neck with the lyrics to the children's song *Old McDonald Had A Farm*. When Mr. McDonald arrived at the store in the morning, Mollie had eaten her way through an entire shelf of potato chips and bags of Reese's Peanut Butter Cups. As punishment for their misdeeds, Marci and her friends had to wash the offensively scented after effects of Mollie's binge eating from the grocery store floors. She claimed it had taken weeks to get the odor of cow manure out of her nose.

One of Marci's favorite stories featured the *capo di tutti capi* who ruled the neighborhood where Cat grew up. His friends called him Blackie, and Cat said she was never sure whether it was due to his unrepentant soul or the god-awful modified afro toupee he always wore.

Cat was quick to point out that Marci would never have known what career path her father's patients had chosen to follow just by looking at them. Sure, there were a few who were caught in a time warp—duck's ass haircuts, tight fitting rolled sleeve tee shirts, cigarettes dangling from their lips and hunks of wire and handguns on their belts. Those visual aids might be dead giveaways, but for the most part, they looked just like everyone else. Quoting Sherlock Holmes, Cat told Marci, "The world is full of obvious things which nobody by any chance ever observes."

"The first time I met Red...," Cat illustrated her point, "... he was standing in our driveway smoking a cigarette. I was returning home from walking, Sheikira, our domesticated wolf, and he stopped me to comment on what an unusual and beautiful animal she was. We talked for a while and, when I finally went into the house, I did so thinking 'What a nice guy. And cute!' After office hours, I mentioned him to my dad. His response was about as curt as one could get. 'Don't ever talk to him again!'"

"Papa bear was protecting his cub. Did you say, 'wolf?'"

"Yes, he was and I did. I know I told you that my parents raised two wolves but that's a story for another day. Let me tell you about Red Richie. Of course, I argued with my dad that Red was '... such a nice guy,' but dad was adamant that I stay far away from him. He even threatened to fire me and make me get a real job. I pressured him to tell me why, and when he finally relented, he said, 'Sure. He's nice... for a hit man.'

I was only 16, but I knew what a hit man was, and I can't say knowing discouraged me in the least. If anything, I was more fascinated and kept hoping that Red would soon need another appointment. Each day when I got home from school, I looked to see if his car was parked in the driveway. Having a home office definitely had its *pros* and *cons*. Pun intended."

"Sounds like you were getting an education on a number of different levels."

"You could say that. A few weeks passed with no sign of Red. Then, one night on the evening news, his face filled the screen. According to the report, he had entered a bar and used a shotgun to blow the heads off a few of the patrons. He was caught by the police a few days later and, at his arraignment, despite handcuffs and shackles, managed to jump through a second story window at the courthouse and escape. The police were asking for help in finding him and a reward was being offered. The last we heard, no one had turned him in."

"Didn't your father feel threatened by these men?"

"Not at all. They knew my dad was a straight up guy. He wanted nothing to do with their lives outside his office. He was there to treat their illnesses and injuries. Nothing else. He never asked questions, and they never offered information. Remember, my father was a police physician. On any given day, there were just as many cops in our waiting room as there were not so law abiding citizens. They all knew each other and, assuming there were no outstanding arrest warrants, they treated each other like long lost friends."

"I guess it was no different than now. We know who the perverts and scumbags are in our community but, without evidence, we can't do a damn thing to put them behind bars."

"Yup. My dad said that he would rather have them sitting in our waiting room than out committing a crime. There were two brothers, soldiers in Blackie's army, who were especially scary—Dennis and John Cafasso. John was the more volatile of the two. In fact, so short was his fuse that he stabbed his brother in the leg over whether or not they should have a July fourth barbeque."

"How serious was the wound?"

"Serious enough that my dad had to drive Dennis to the hospital. Of course, Dennis didn't want to get his brother in any trouble so he told the emergency room doctor that he had cut himself on a piece of broken glass. Dad said it was obvious the doctor didn't believe his story, but... well, he was smart enough to just stitch the wound and send Dennis home. The next day, they were acting like nothing had happened.

A few months later, John got injured on the job—his legitimate job. The brothers owned a wholesale beverage company and sold large quantities of beer and soft drinks for parties and public events. He came into my dad's office complaining that he had excruciating pain in his back, neck and shoulders. He wanted to file a workman's comp case and needed an attorney.

Dad never liked to recommend one particular lawyer over another even if he felt he or she was best for the case. That way, if the case did not settle in favor of a patient, dad could not be held responsible."

"But your dad wouldn't be responsible one way or the other."

"You know that and I know that, but we're not talking about reasonable and rational people here, especially in John Cafasso's case. Dad avoided offering suggestions by giving anyone who asked for references the names of a few attorneys we trusted, showing no preference for any one man. The lawyer John choose, however, happened to be my dad's best friend."

"Smart move but I get the feeling things didn't go well."

"The case proceeded to arbitration, but John was not satisfied with the amount of money offered. He insisted on going to court and totally disregarded his attorney's warning that the insurance company would waste no effort in proving his injuries less severe than he claimed.

Came the day of the trial and, sure enough, the lawyers for the insurance company produced a video of John carrying heavy wooden crates of soda bottles and kegs of beer. Bye, bye settlement. He was angry, but he was angry with the attorney, not himself.

In a fit of temper, John stormed into dad's office and threatened to kill his friend. Knowing that John kept a baseball bat that he had sawed into a club in his car, Dad kept him calm by offering him a drink. While getting that drink, he called Blackie and advised him of the situation. At his request, John was kept occupied until he arrived.

Watching someone get the shit kicked out of him in the movies is nothing like watching in real life. There's no slow motion. Things happens so quickly that you can neither prepare yourself nor get out of the way. Just as John was taking a sip of his drink,

Blackie walked up behind him and hit him so hard in the back of the head that the glass broke and cut into the bridge of his nose. With blood streaming down his face, Blackie lifted John out of his chair by the shirt and delivered a few well-placed punches to his stomach and chin. Then, with John dazed and bleeding, Blackie warned him, 'If one hair on that attorney's head is out of place, this is nothing compared to what I will do to you. Get the hell out of my sight.'"

"John didn't fight back? Didn't argue with Blackie?"

"Nope. Nobody argued with Blackie. Not if they valued their life. The Hammer escorted John out of the office. Blackie extended a hand in thanks to my dad and left. We never saw John again, but we did hear stories... scary stories that I won't repeat just in case he's still alive and knows how to use Google maps.

"Crap!"

"Now, just so you don't get the wrong impression, we had many more average patients than we did strange characters. Side by side in the waiting room, they shared stories of spouses, kids, pets and everyday life. Anyone listening would never know the difference between them. That's why I always tell people that there is a real danger in talking to strangers."

Donna M. Carbone

Made in the USA
Charleston, SC
28 April 2016